Adams County Wedding

Volume 1, Number 1, Fall 2015

In this issue

We love where we live— Adams County, Pennsylvania

Our Cover is Miranda and Andy's wedding at Beech Springs Farm by Gary Wilkinson.

All photographs and text in this issue were produced by Susan and David Bonser except where credited. Individual content owners reserve all rights ©2015. Write to us at PO Box 204, Aspers, PA 17304 or email susan@adamscw.com

Adams County Wedding will be published periodically, perhaps quarterly, as a labor of love. The digital edition is free. A print version of each issue is available from Amazon (search Adams County Wedding). *Our website*: adamscw.com
Instagram.com/adamscountywedding
Facebook.com/adamscountywedding

Weddings...

It's all about love. The magical time of finding that special other person whose puzzle piece fits yours perfectly. It is a most incredible time of life—and then you get to have a great party to celebrate your happiness with all of your favorite family and friends. What could be better? I know some people will say "elope." And we love that idea, too. This magazine is all about how people tie the knot in Adams County, Pennsylvania. What we have learned in creating just this first issue is that there are extraordinarily talented people, amazing venues, and great support here for wedding in Adams County.

If this is the first time you have seen us, we will publish several times a year and share our magazine online without charge. We focus on the traditions, the talented people, and wonderful celebrations of marriage that take place in Adams County, Pennsylvania. Tell us your wedding story. We'd love to feature it here!

Susan & David Bonser

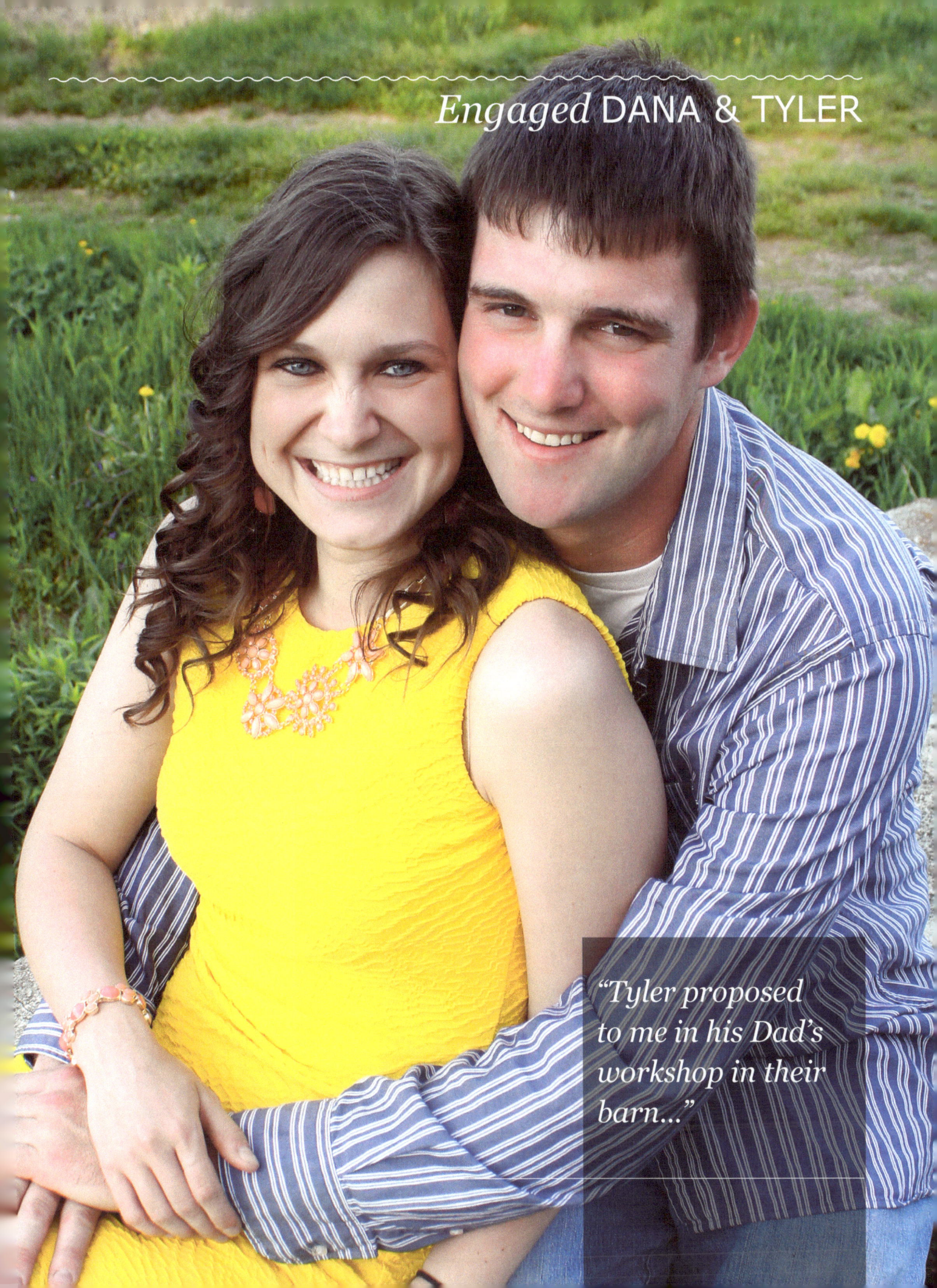

"Tyler proposed to me in his Dad's workshop in their barn..."

Photographed by Jordan Soliday

Dana and Tyler met when they were ten years old at 4-H camp. (She thanks her Aunt who is an extension agent in the 4-H Clubs of Adams County.) Both grew up in local families. Dana's brother and father operate Group Orchards in Gardners and Tyler comes from Lagging Stream Farm, a family-owned dairy farm. They were friends throughout their school years, seeing each other at 4-H fairs and events, but lost touch when high school ended.

After college, Tyler and Dana met again in Gettysburg. Tyler had completed a degree in Residential Construction Management at Pennsylvania College of Technology and Dana had earned her degree in nursing at Penn State University. She works now at Wellspan in Gettysburg and told us, "I love our rural, local down-to-earth area. The patients I see and take care of are so appreciative and make my job so rewarding."

Tyler was refinishing a piece of antique furniture for Dana. It had once belonged to her grandmother. He used to take Dana to his father's workshop in their barn to show her the progress he was making on it. Dana told us, "On Thanksgiving it was no different. We went into the shop and he showed me how it was coming along. I opened one of the doors in the piece of furniture. He had put the ring inside with 'Will you Marry Me?' written on a piece of paper."

Dana was surprised and said, "Yes." She and Tyler had talked about getting engaged—though she was not expecting it at that moment. Tyler is renovating property subdivided off the orchard for their new home. Both of them expressed gratitude to their parents and cherish their families. Dana explained, "We have had parents that have shaped and guided us and they continue to do so in this next step we are taking."

Congratulations and much happiness to you both!

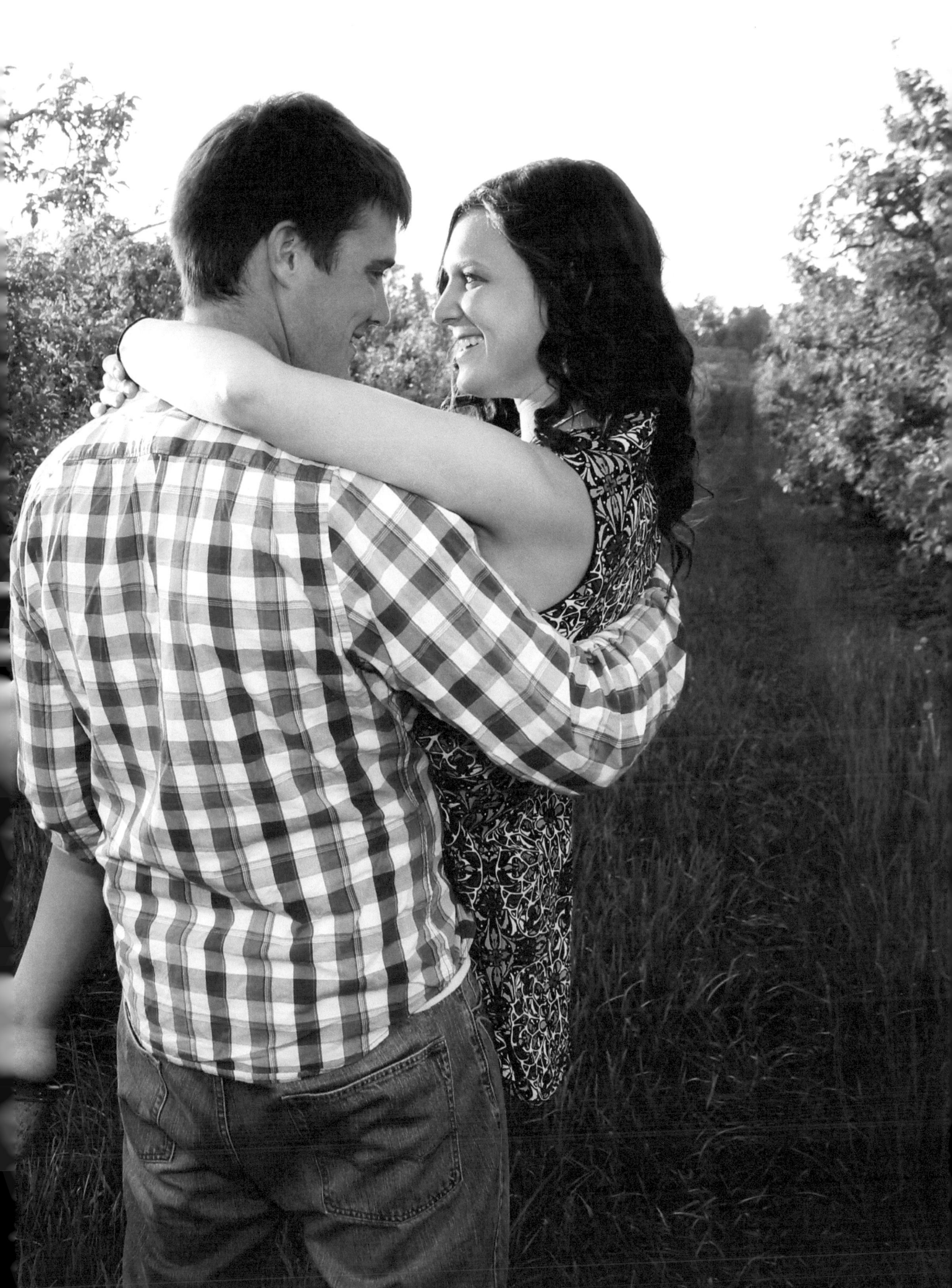

Wedding MIRANDA AND ANDY

Photographed by Gary Wilkinson

Miranda and Andy met at a summer cookout on the Susquehanna River. "A few weekends later we went on our first date, hit it off, and the rest is history," Miranda told us. They were both from York County, so once they decided to get married they began to look for their perfect place to have the wedding. They knew they wanted to have it at a barn and started visiting locations.

Miranda and Andy chose to have their wedding ceremony in the garden and the reception in the barn. Andy's Aunt Darla and Uncle Don showed them a creative idea for the ceremony using antique doors with painted scripture across a lintel. The couple loved the idea and chose the verse, telling us "we felt it was simple but powerful." Search wedding doors online to see more ways couples are using antique doors in weddings.

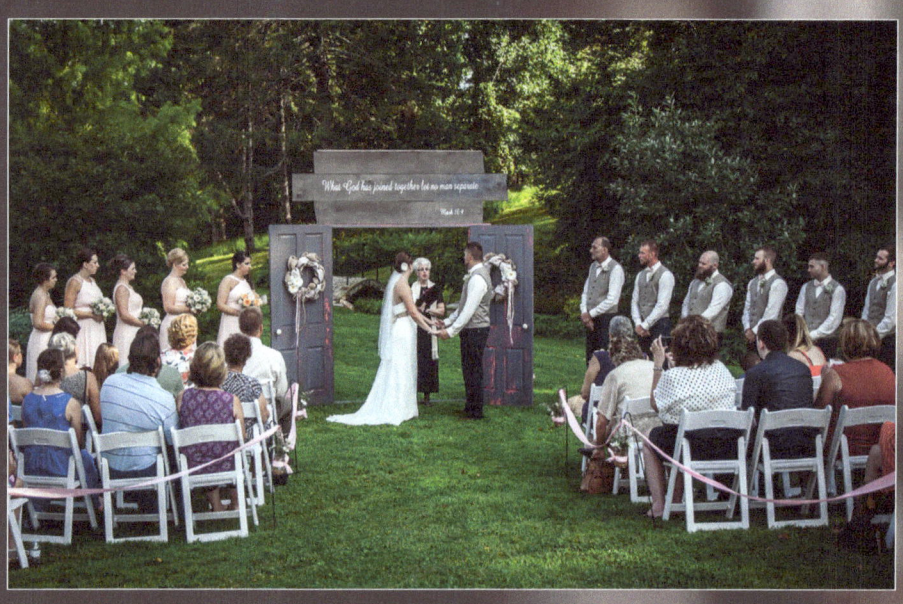

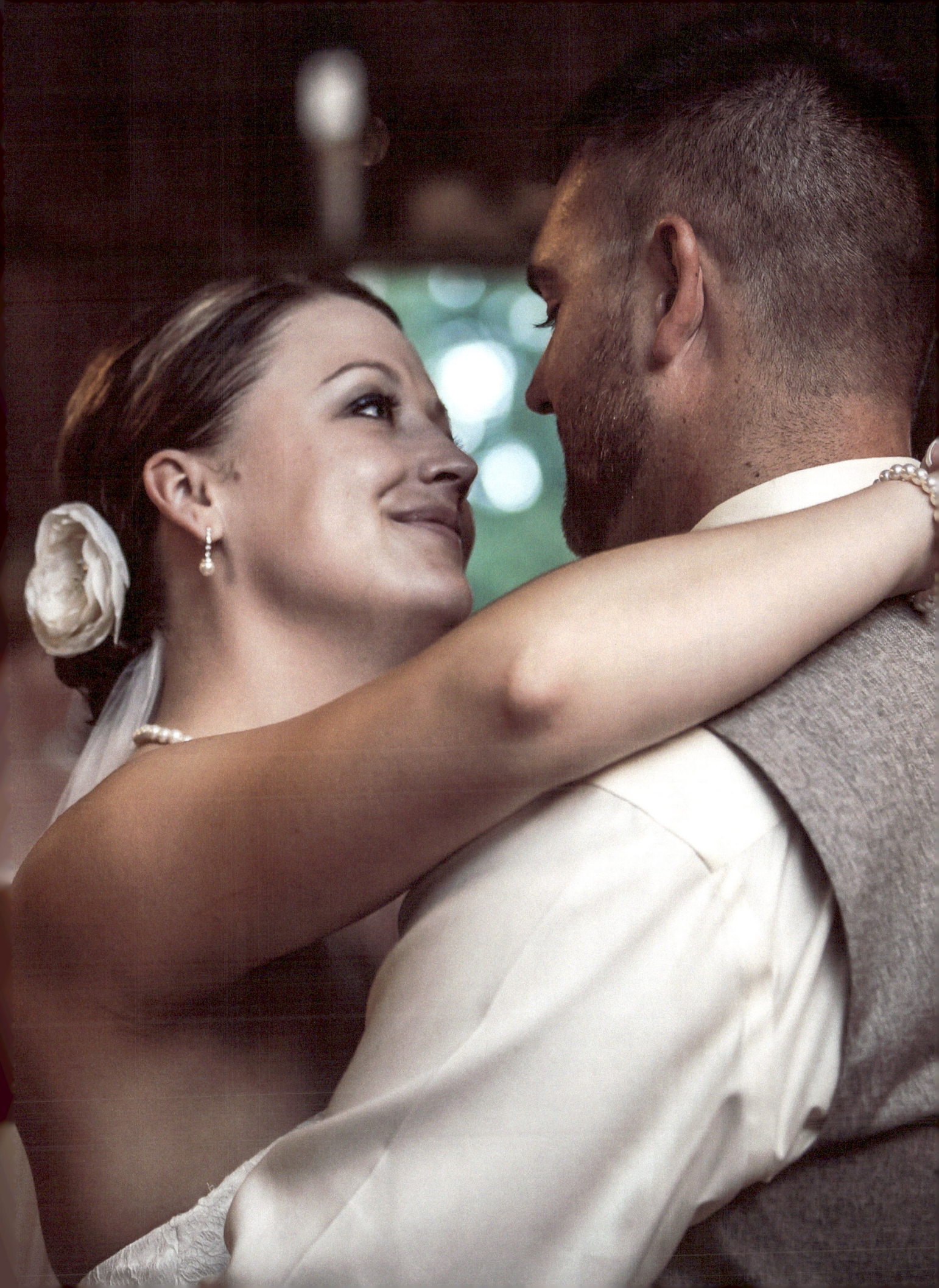

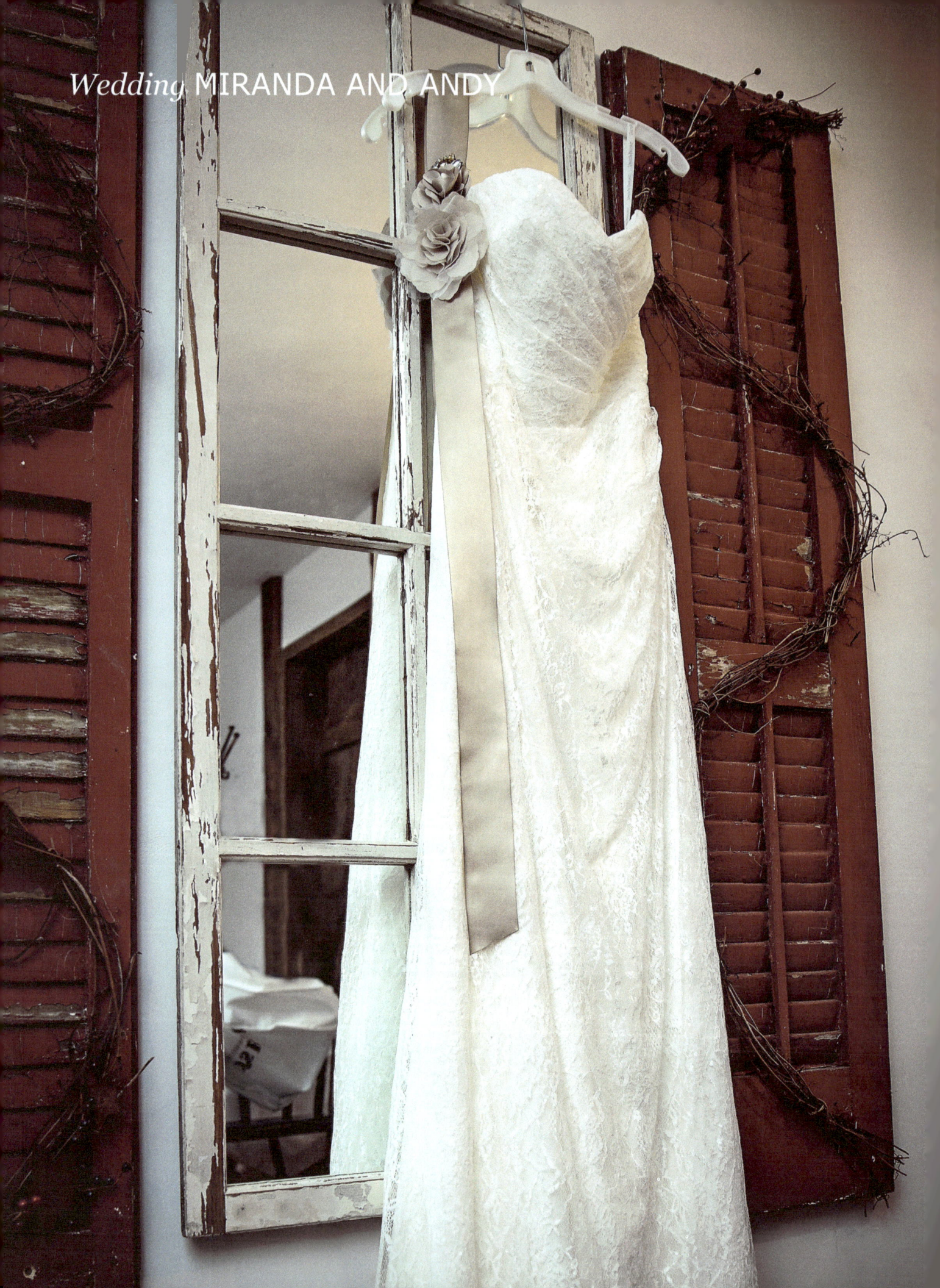

They found their venue, Beech Springs Farm in Adams County, on RusticBride.com. Miranda said, "As soon as we visited the farm and met Jayne we fell in love. The property was beautiful, we loved its history, we felt comfortable and at home here."

Miranda also knew she wanted a lace gown or to at least have lace on her gown. She loves the vintage, rustic look of lace. When she found her sash, she fell in love with it. "I got that 'I feel beautiful' feeling," Miranda told us.

Their most memorable moment of the wedding? "For both of us it was when we recited the vows that we wrote for each other," they told us.

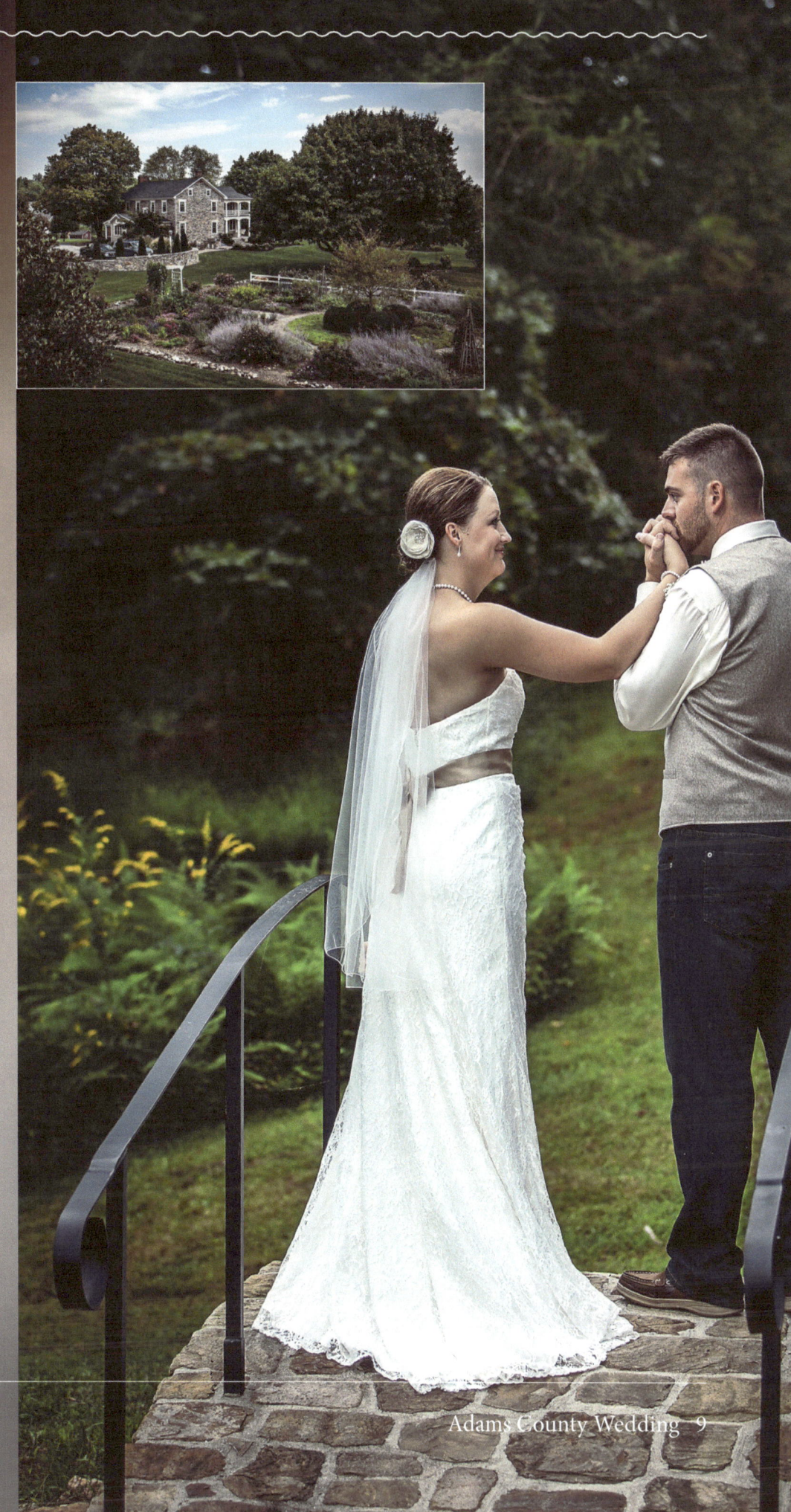

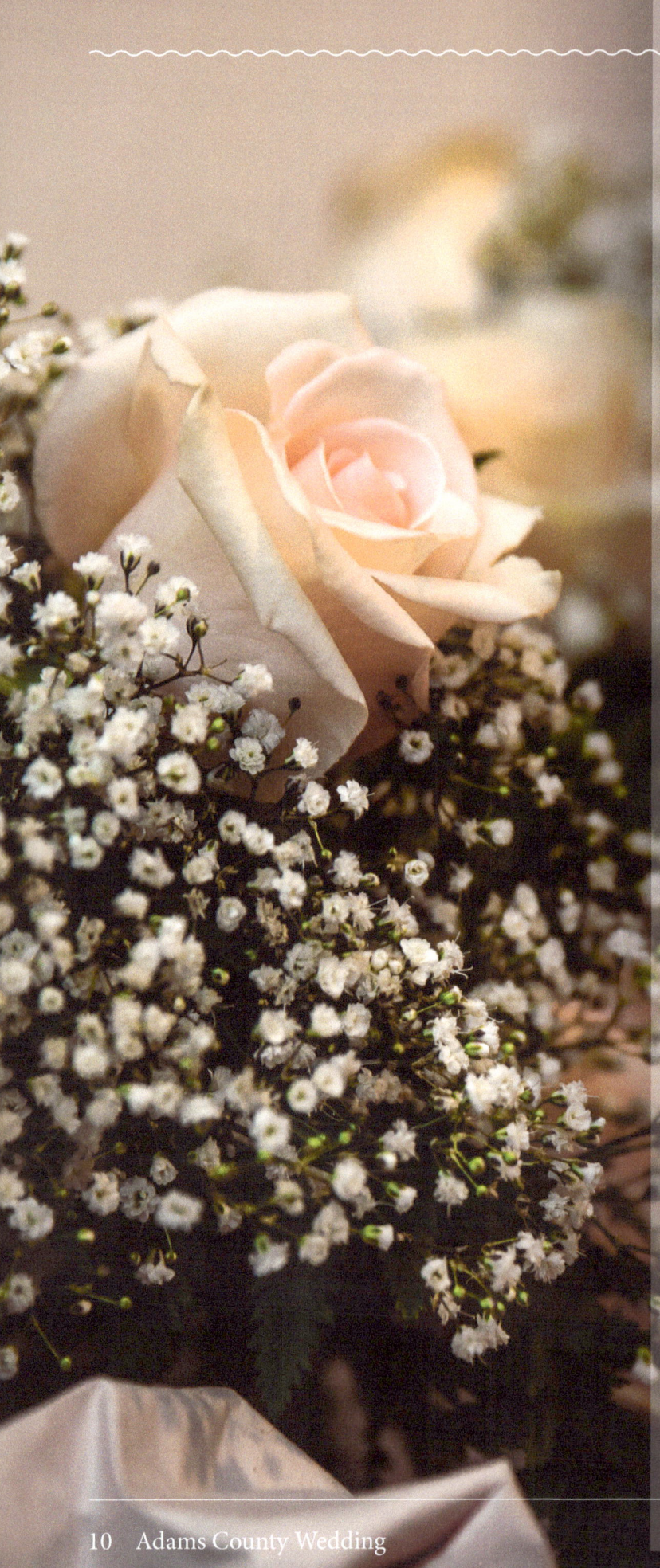

Miranda had her bride and bridesmaid bouquets created by the Golden Carriage in Dover. She chose roses and baby's breath in classic round posey bouquets. The colors of her flowers ranged from darker hues of coral to pale pink and ivory. The bridesmaids carried the lighter color bouquets which complimented their pale pink dresses.

She had two cake toppers made for the wedding—one to cut in the cake ceremony and one to save for their first anniversary.

The table centerpieces were put together by their family on the day of rehearsal. The family floral designers put together different set ups for them to chose from. "Andy and I really liked the wild flower look," Miranda explained.

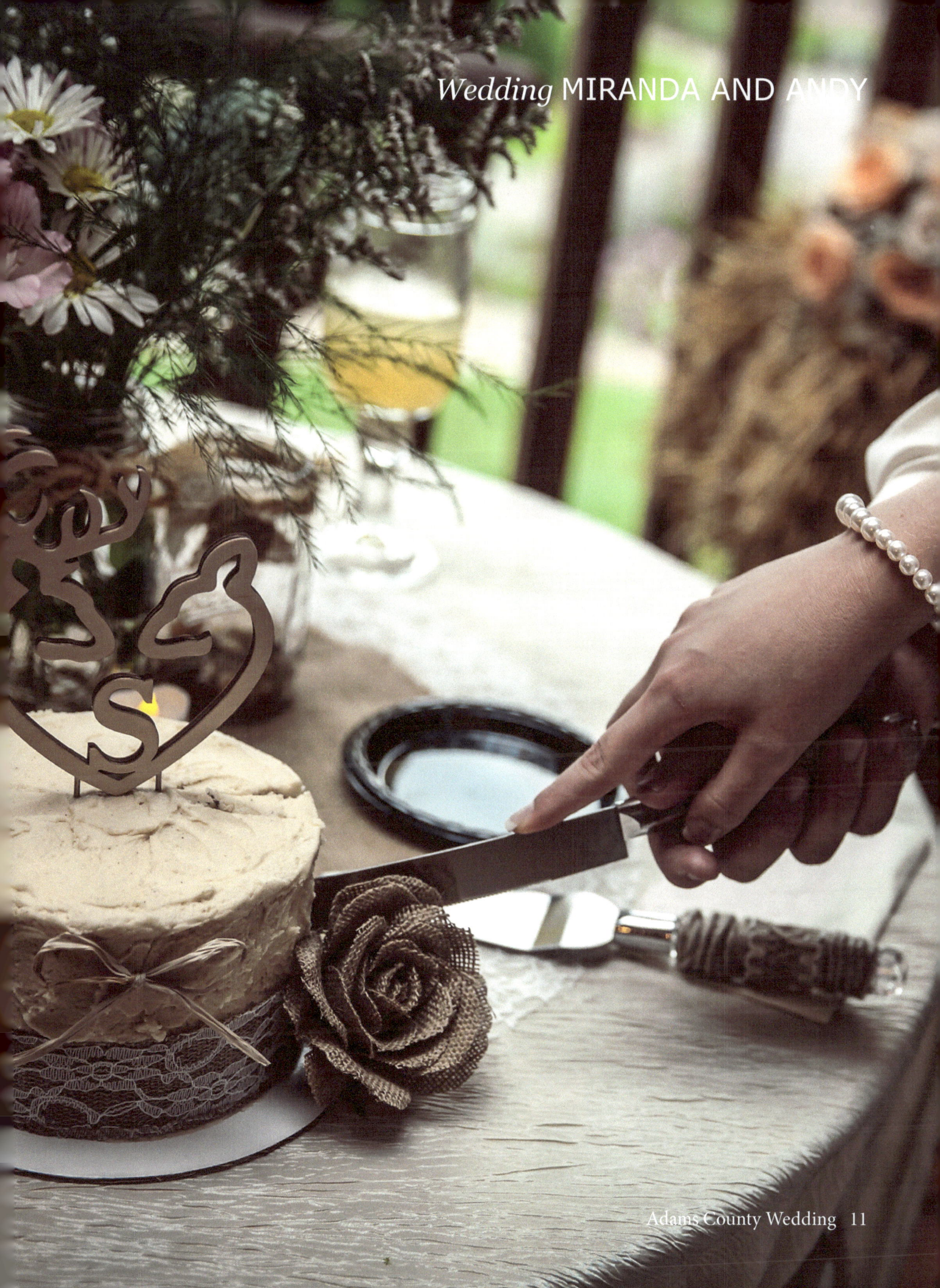

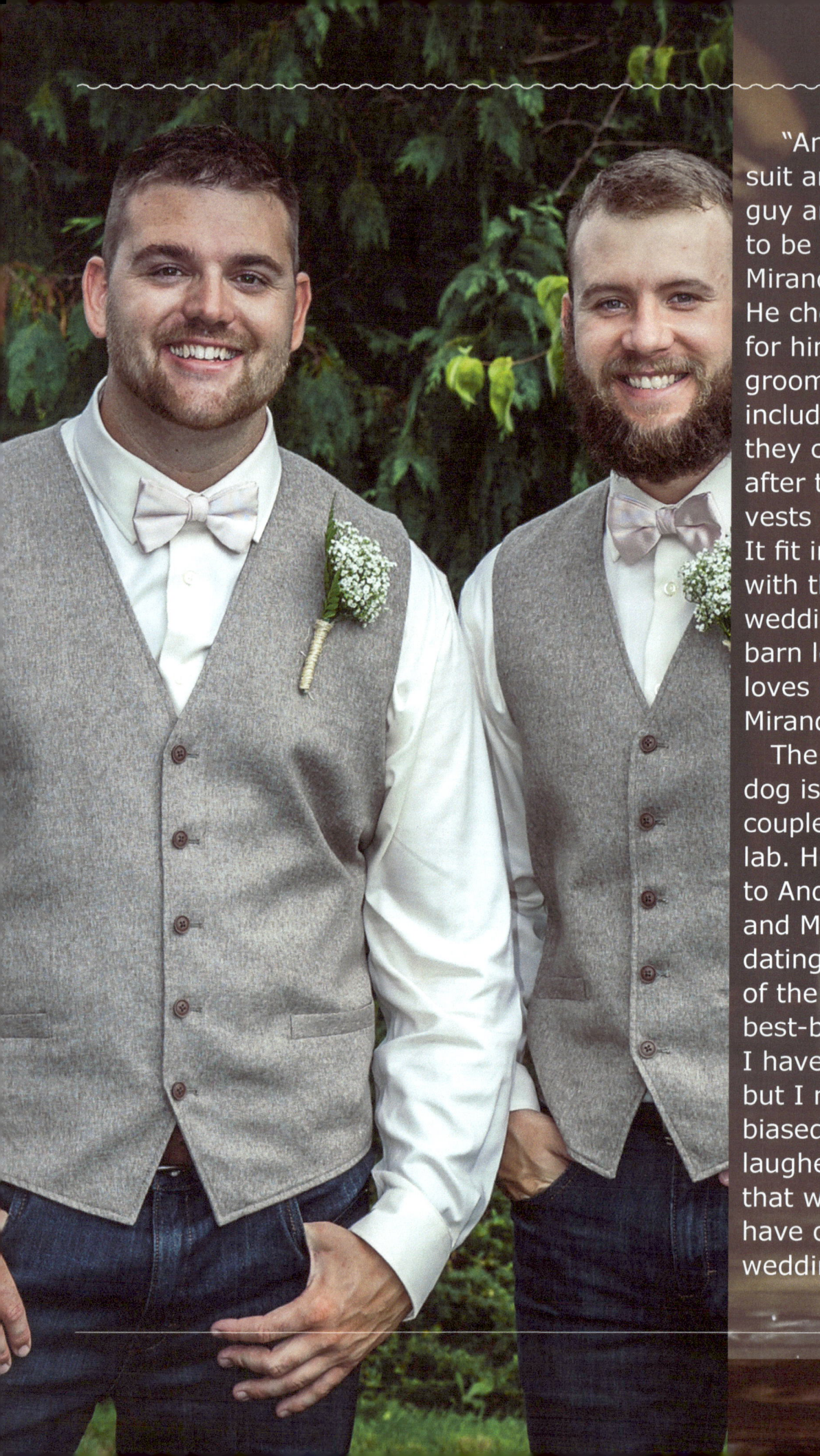

"Andy is not a suit and tie kind of guy and he wanted to be comfortable," Miranda told us. He chose a look for himself and his groomsmen that included jeans (that they could wear after the wedding), vests and bowties. It fit in perfectly with the rustic wedding theme and barn location. "Andy loves bowties," Miranda explained.

The beautiful dog is Bailey, the couple's yellow lab. He belonged to Andy before he and Miranda started dating. "He is one of the smartest and best-behaved dogs I have ever seen... but I may be a little biased." Miranda laughed, "We love that we were able to have our dog at our wedding!"

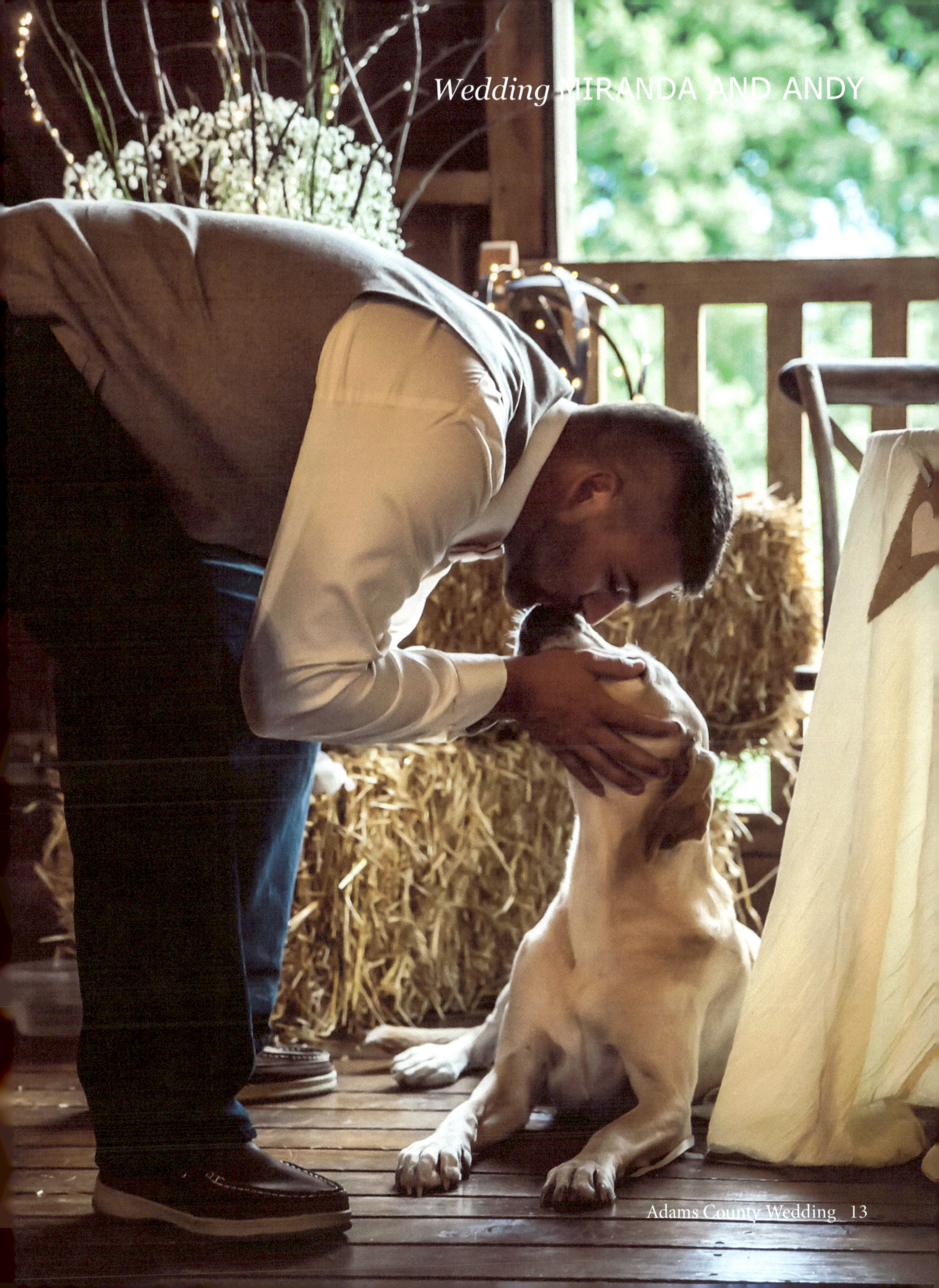

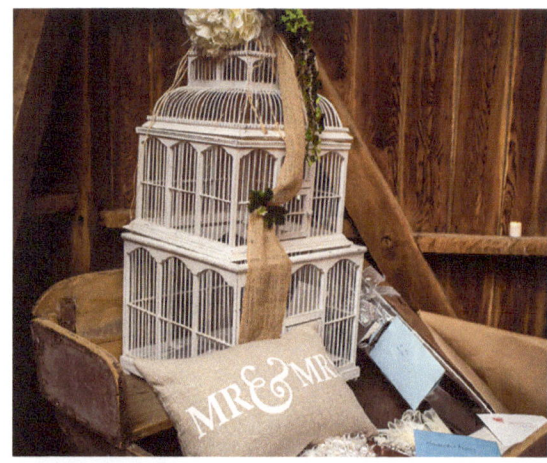

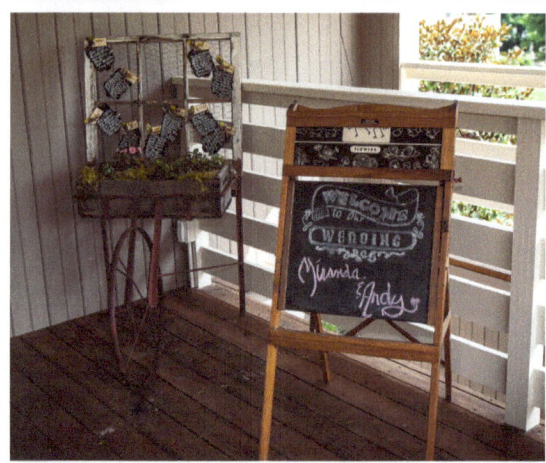

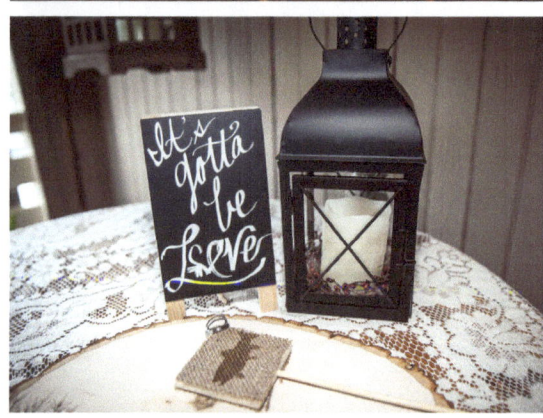

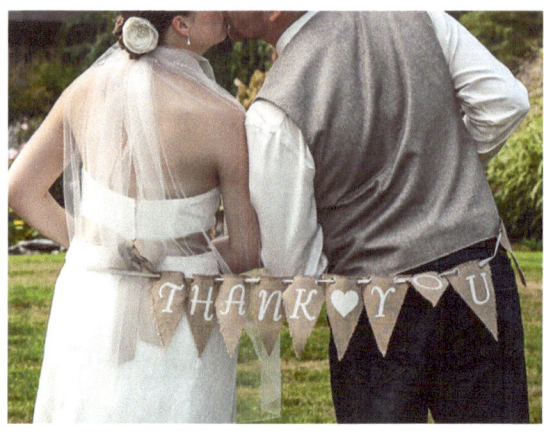

Miranda's advice for brides, "I try to tell other brides to relax, try not to stress the small things, and take it all in on your wedding day. If something goes wrong don't sweat it. In the end you get to marry your best friend!"

Their family was an integral part of planning and putting everything together. Family and friends hand-crafted the wedding doors, the wildflower arrangements, and calligraphy for the table assignments to just name a few of their creative contributions.

Miranda and Andy's goal for their wedding was "Family, simplicity, country, laid back, and fun party." It looks like they achieved all of that.

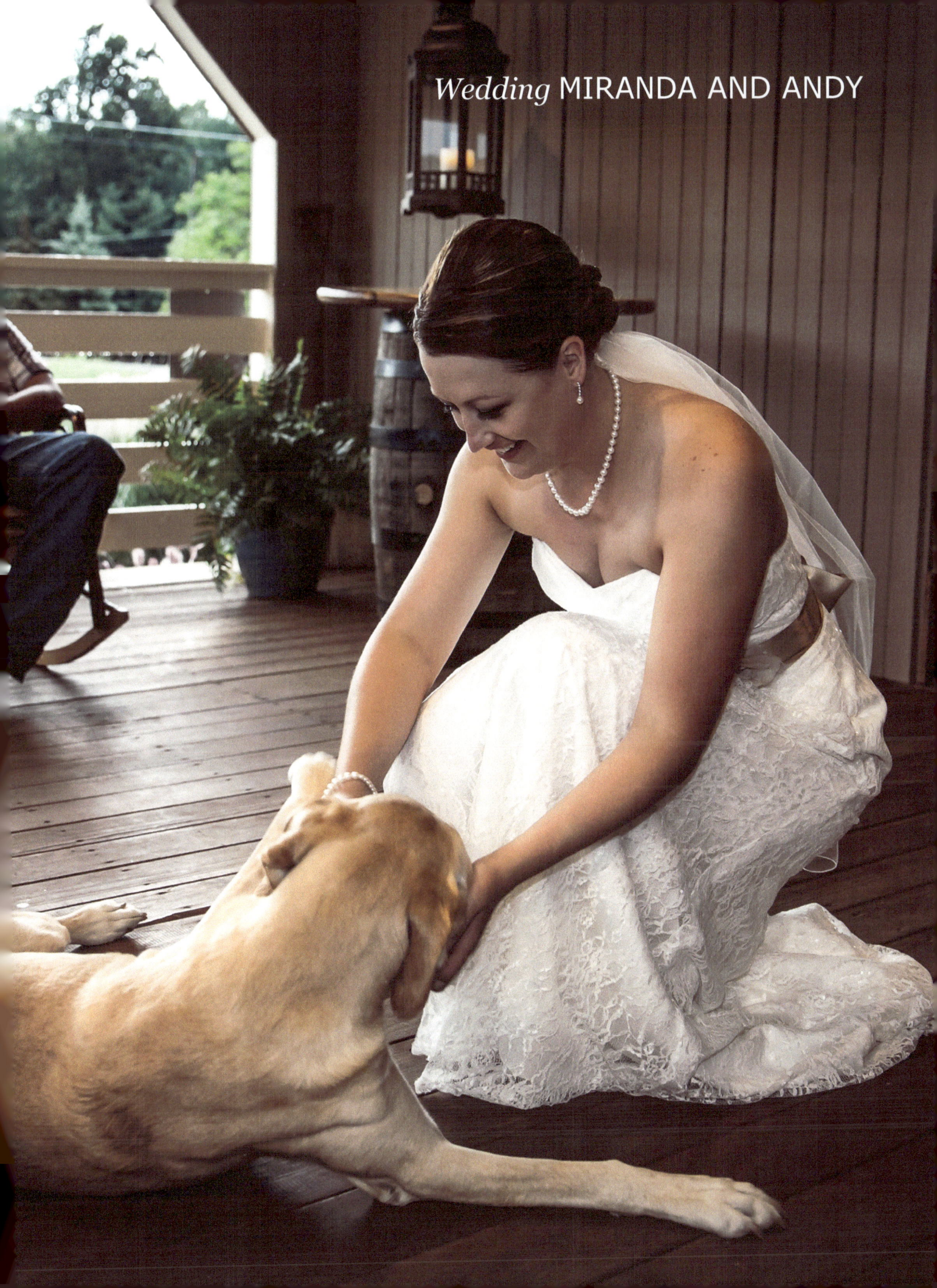

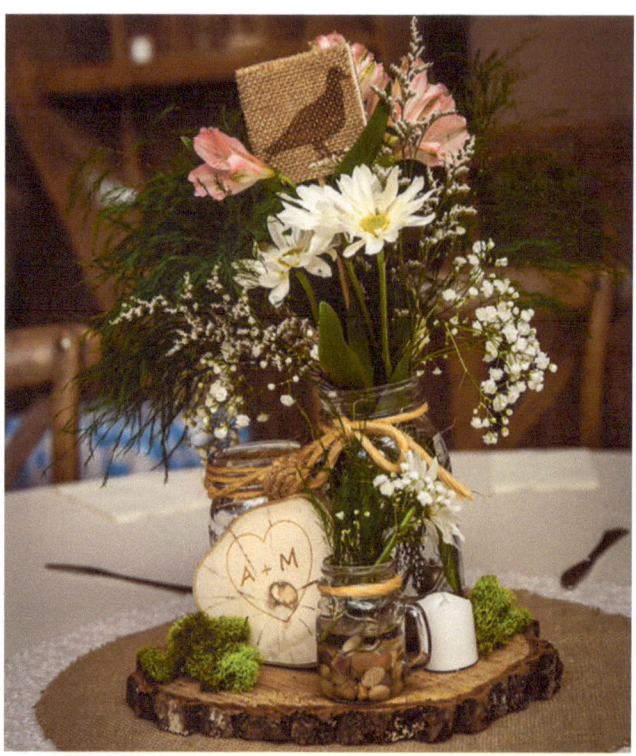

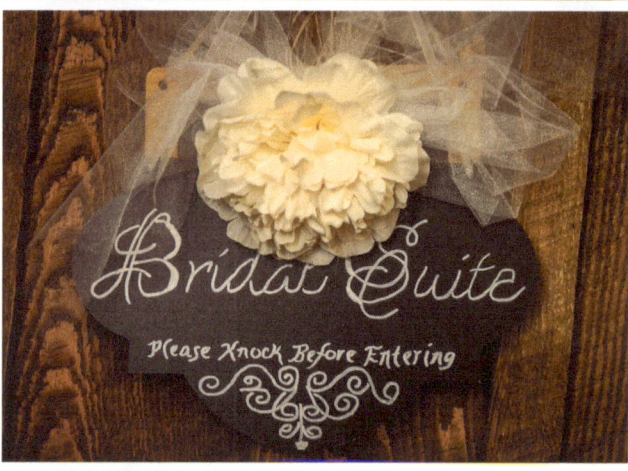

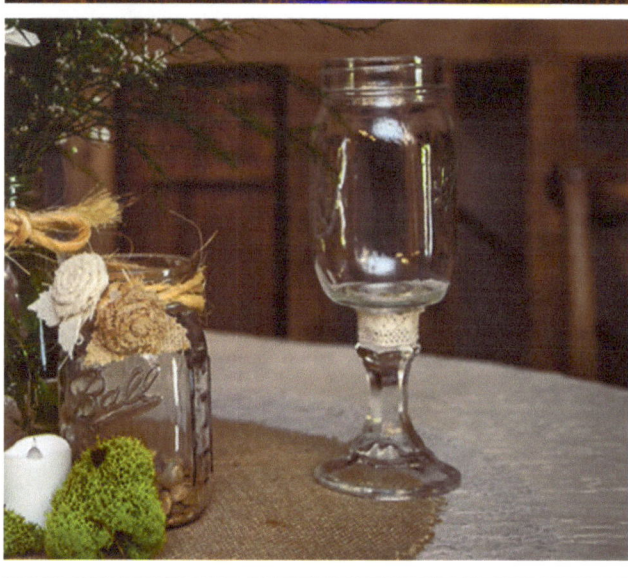

Putting together all of the details of a wedding can be fun. Miranda said she spent a lot of time sifting ideas at Pinterest and Etsy. She told us, "I found a lot of great ideas that could be done ourselves without spending tons of money."

She found a slice of wood that was used as a guest book for everyone to sign. After the wedding, the couple hung it in their house.

Canning jars were used as candleholders, stemware, and decoration. They can be found for sale or make your own following YouTube tutorials.

Right, Bailey snuggled with, "my niece Emma. She looked so cute in her dress that day!"

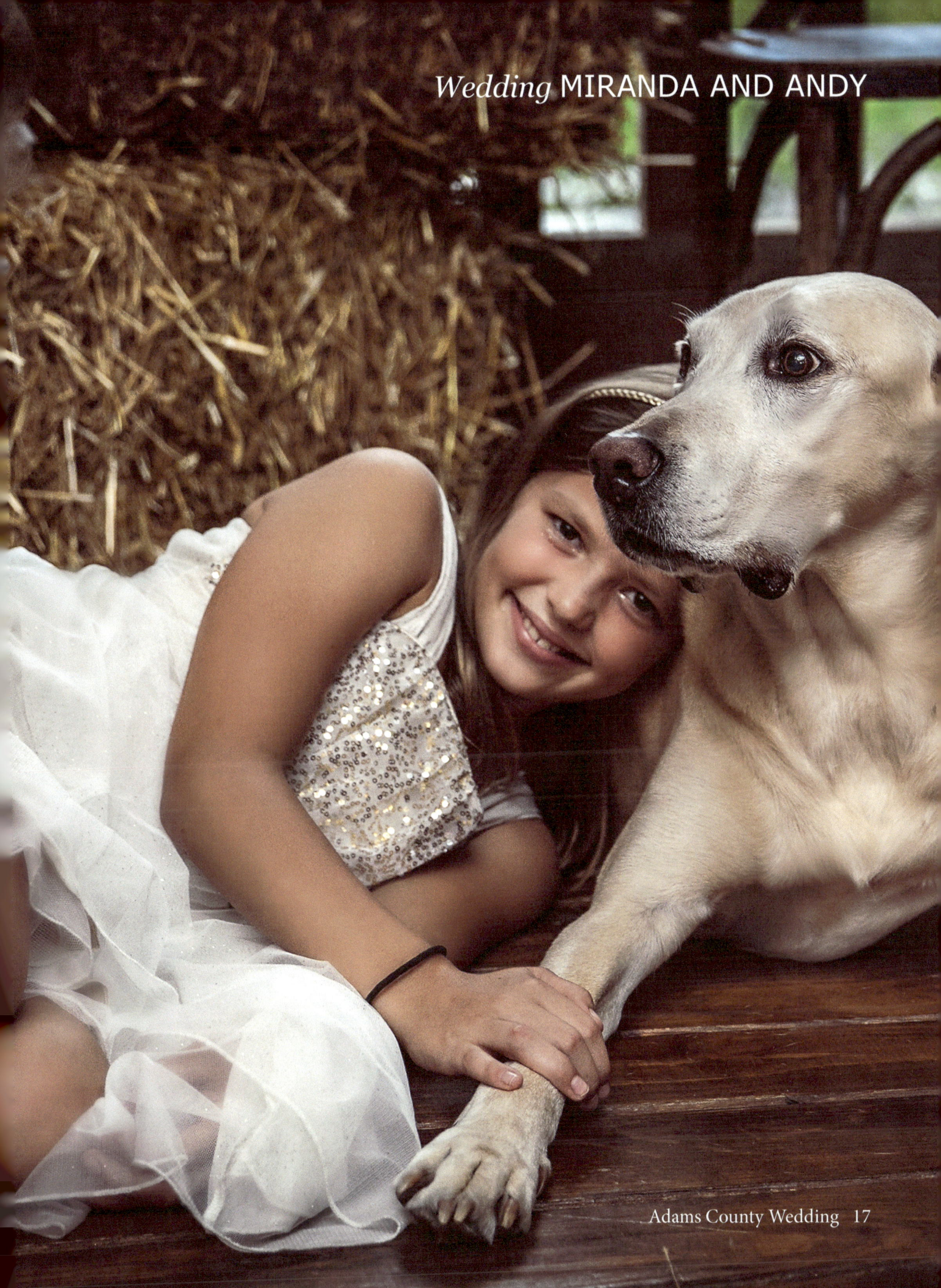

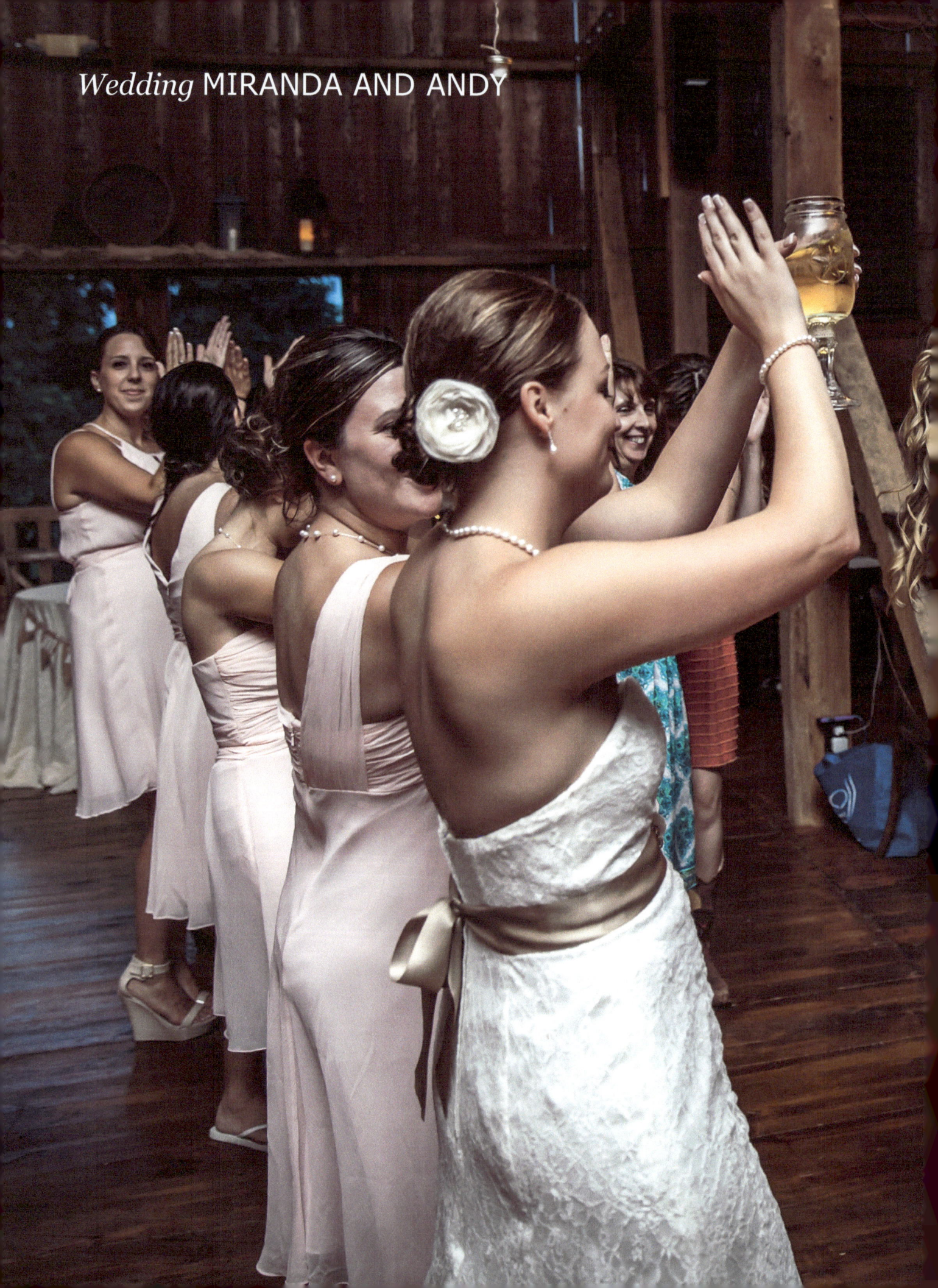

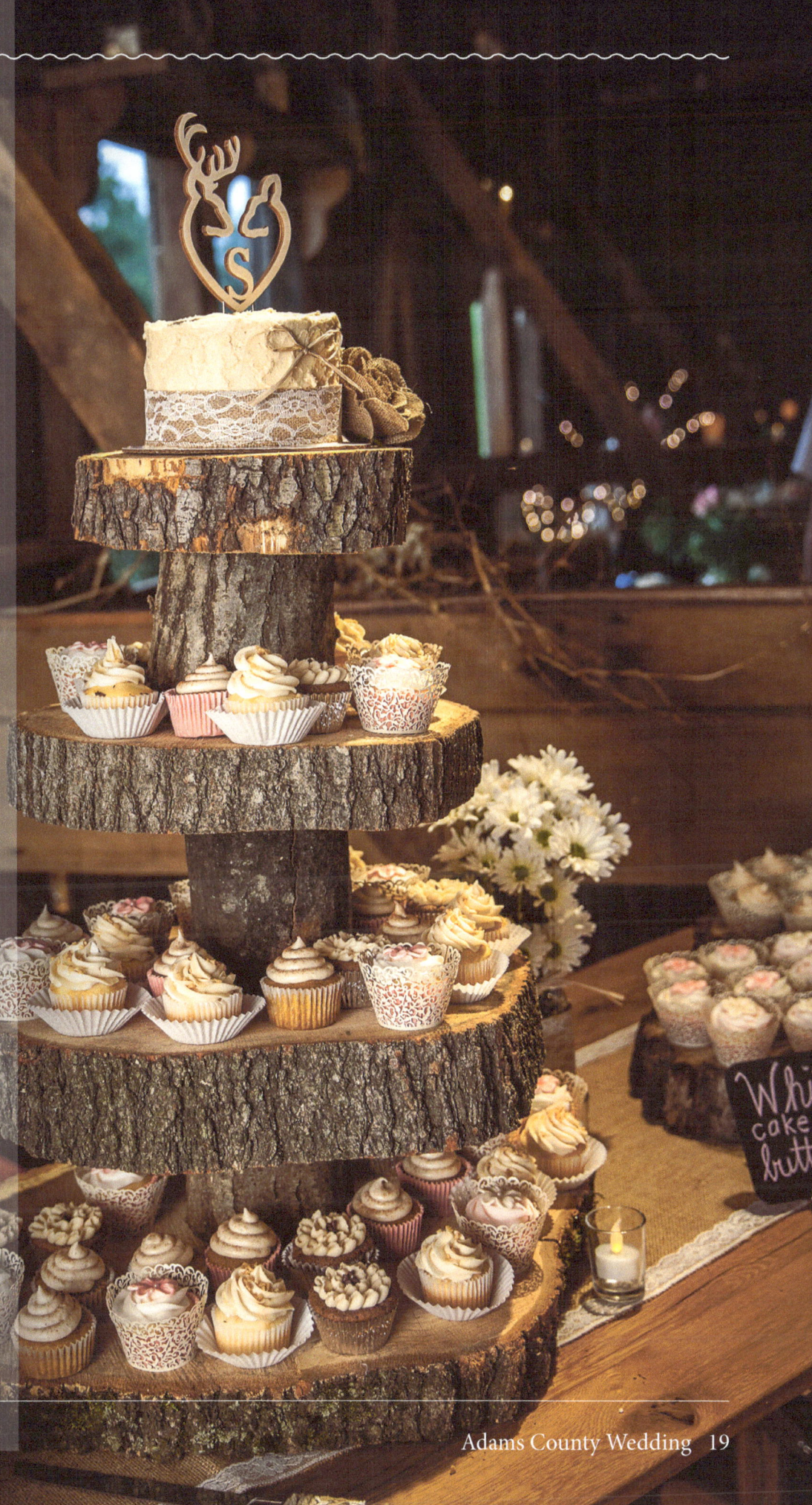

Miranda and Andy decided to have cupcakes for their guests. She told us, "they were from Crème de la Cakes made by Jennifer Horn. Jennifer is the daughter of the owners of Beech Spring Farms. The cupcakes were amazing! We had four different flavors and our guests still talk about the how good they were!"

Another popular idea is rustic slices of wood made into a cupcake serving stand. Do-it-your-selfers will find instructions on Pinterest, can purchase one on Etsy or even rent one locally.

Left, it wouldn't be a barn party without a line dance!

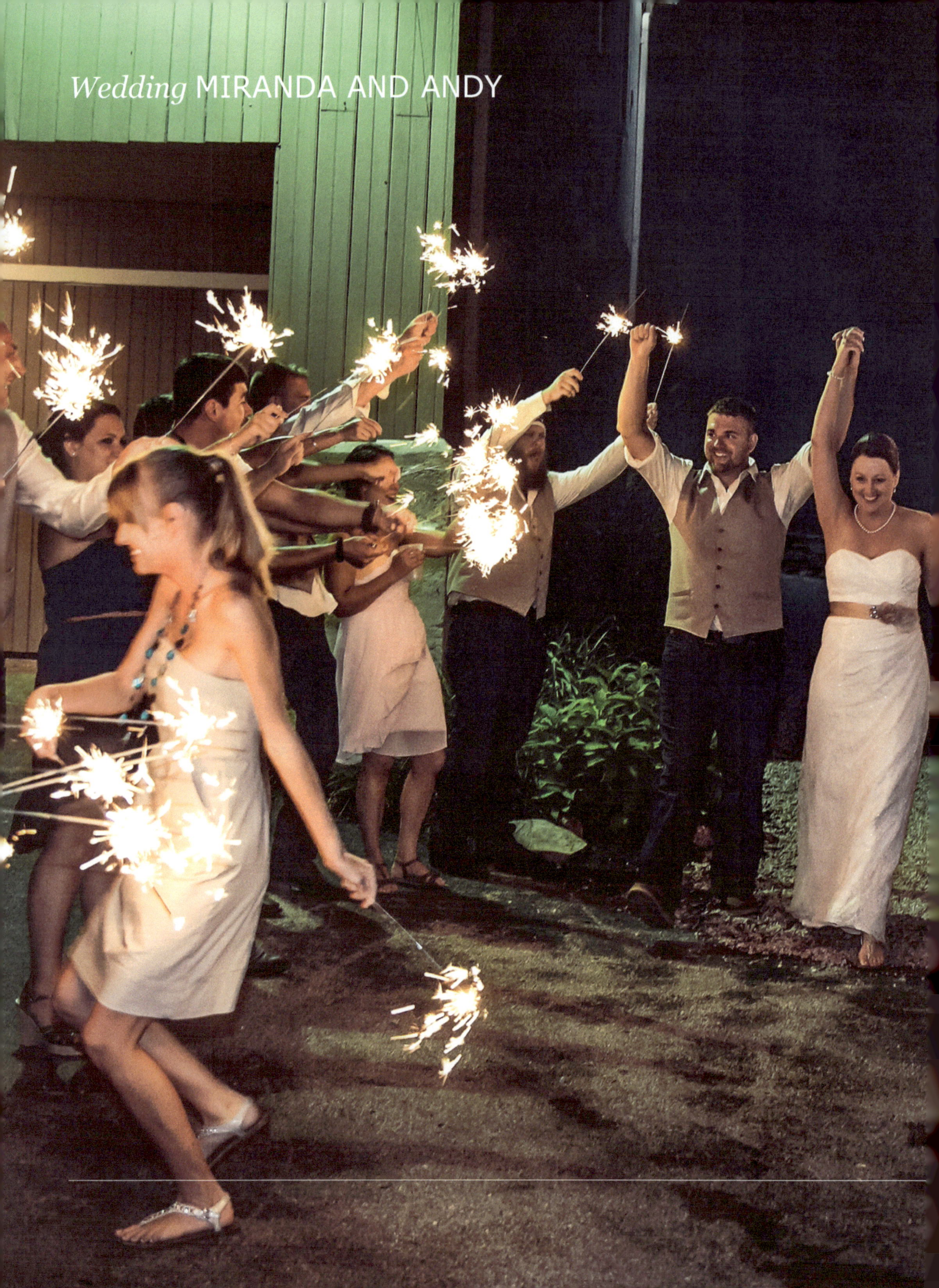

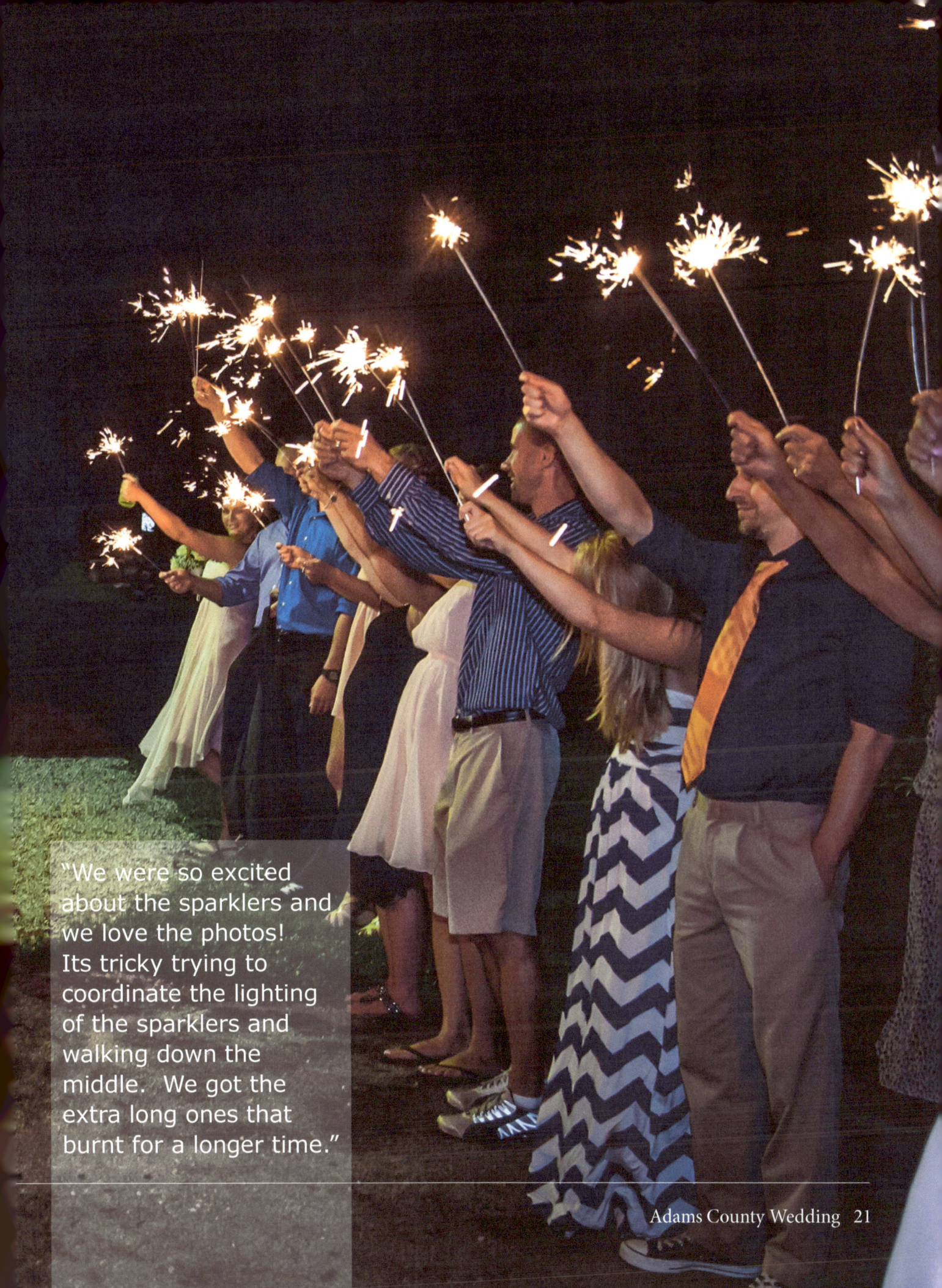

"We were so excited about the sparklers and we love the photos! Its tricky trying to coordinate the lighting of the sparklers and walking down the middle. We got the extra long ones that burnt for a longer time."

Wedding Flowers FOREVER MEMORIES

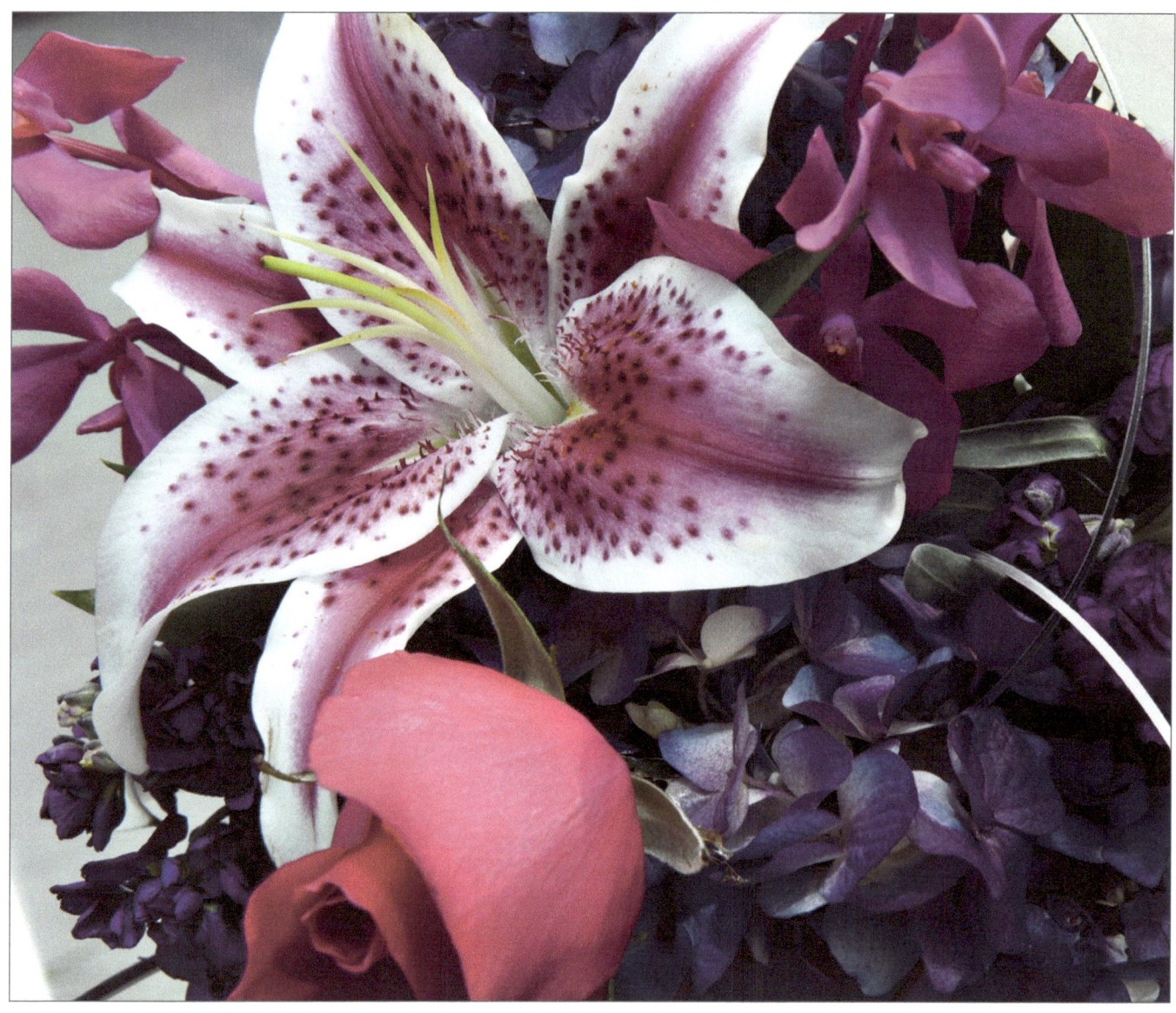

Photographed by Leer Photography

Elegant. When you walk into the room and the flowers are stunning it can take your breath away. Roses have the power to do that. Lillies can be knockout gorgeous. Rich colors like fuscia and purple can make you say "Wow". A beautiful little girl dressed like a princess, making a path of fragrant rose petals for the bride. This is the stuff of fairytales and forever memories.

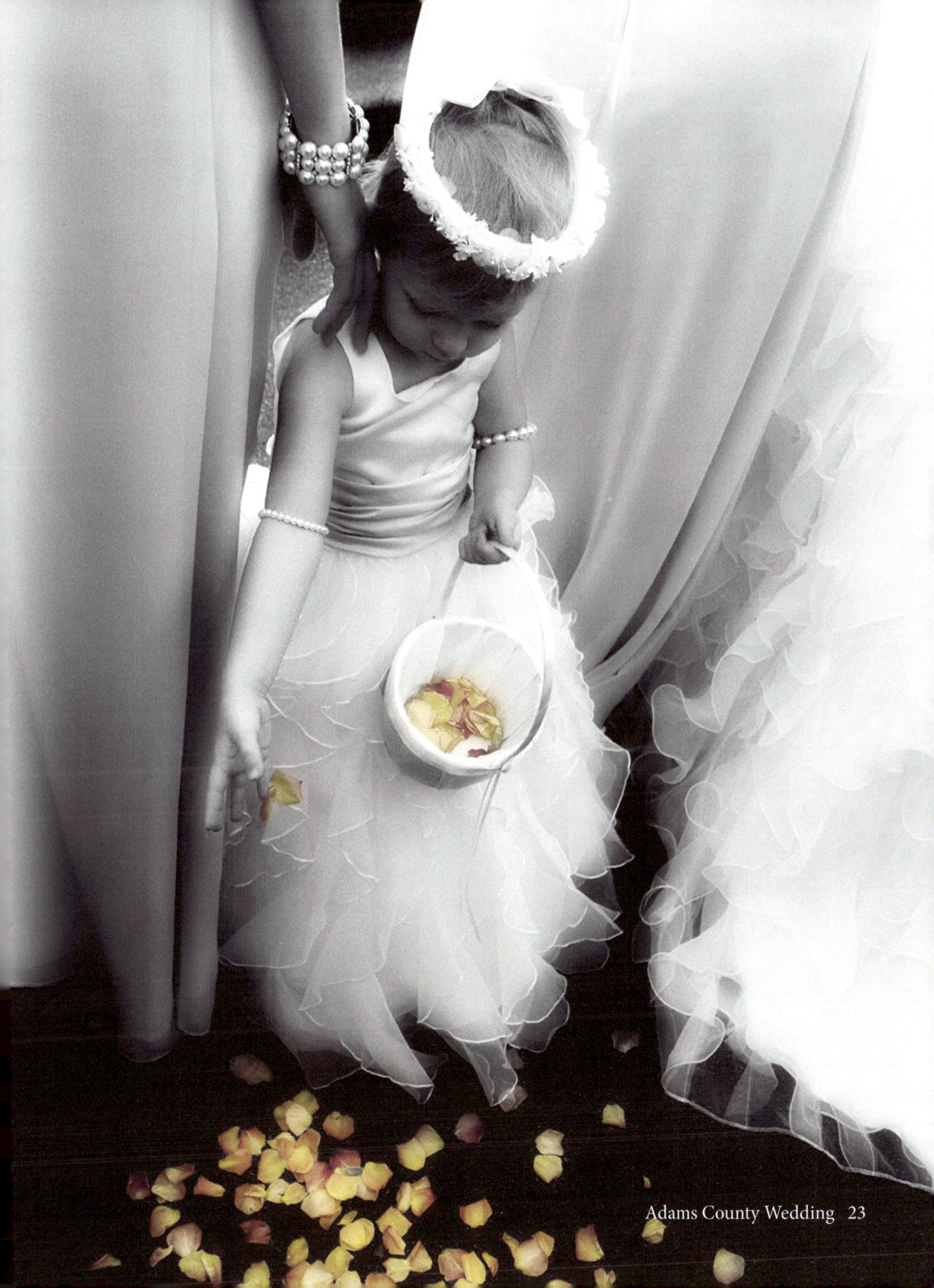

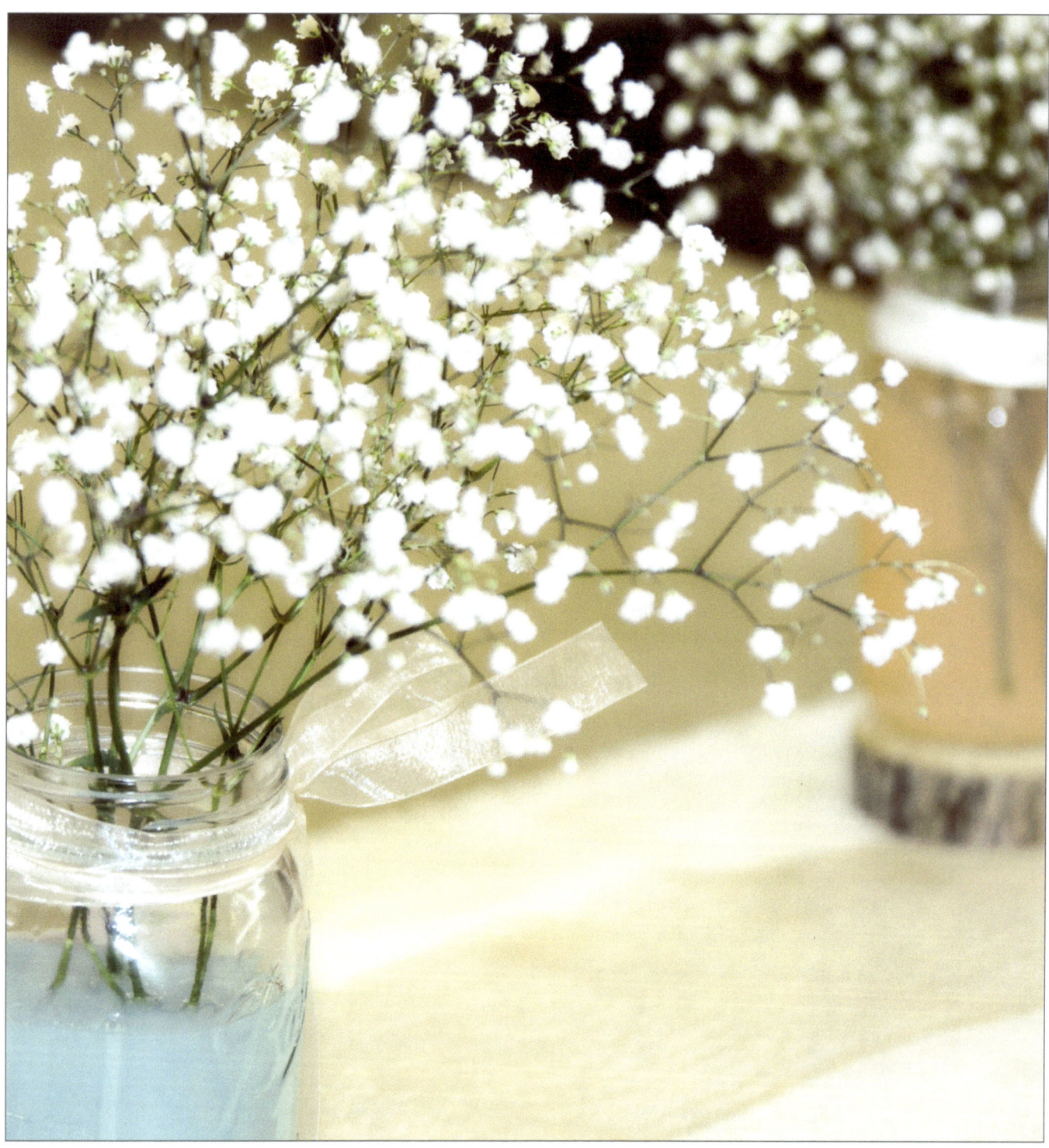

Simplicity. The joy of baby's breath, daisies, the color white, mason jars, natural wood. The appeal is understandable. These are the things we grew up with, cherished—and are wedding trending today.

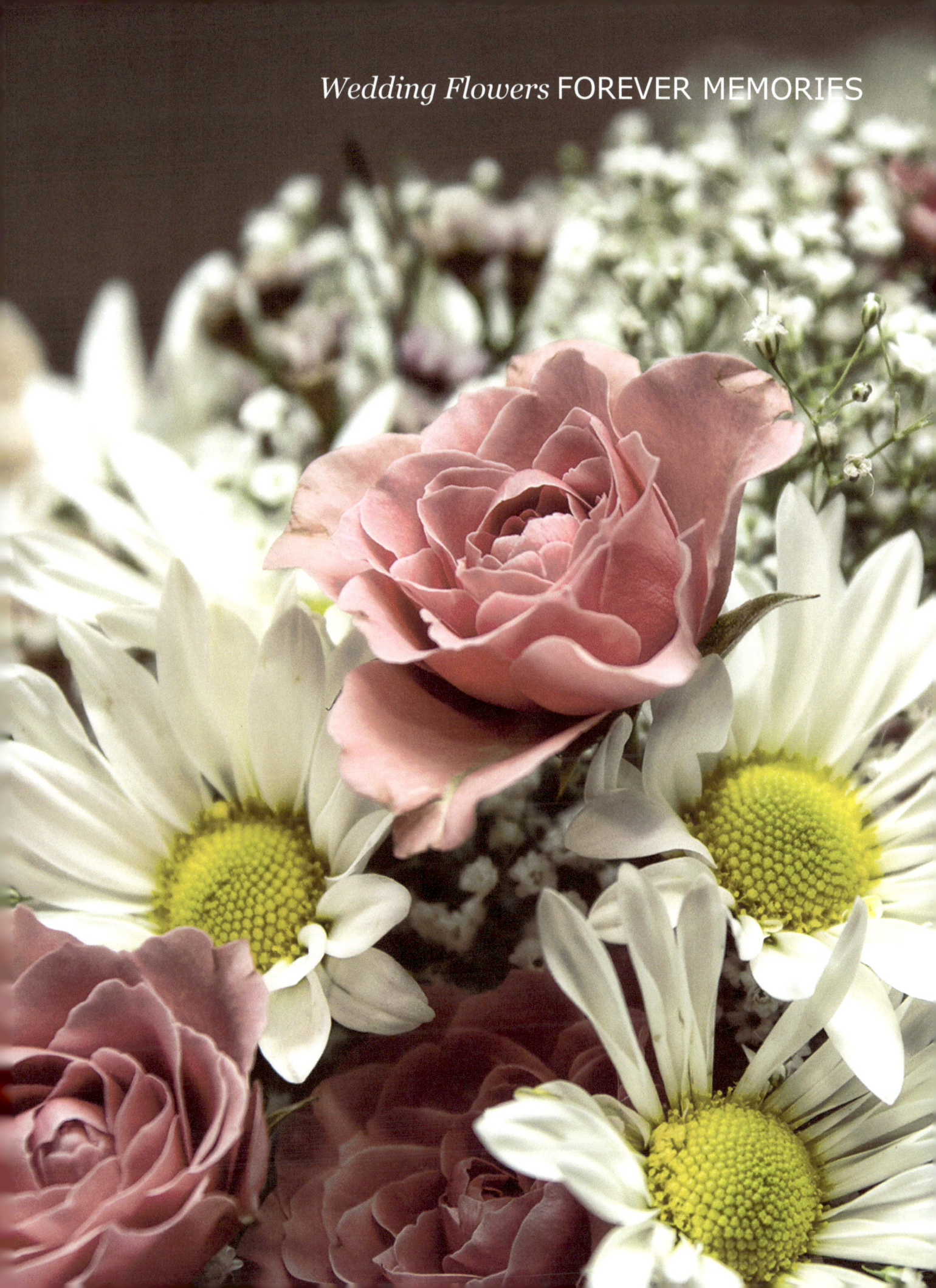

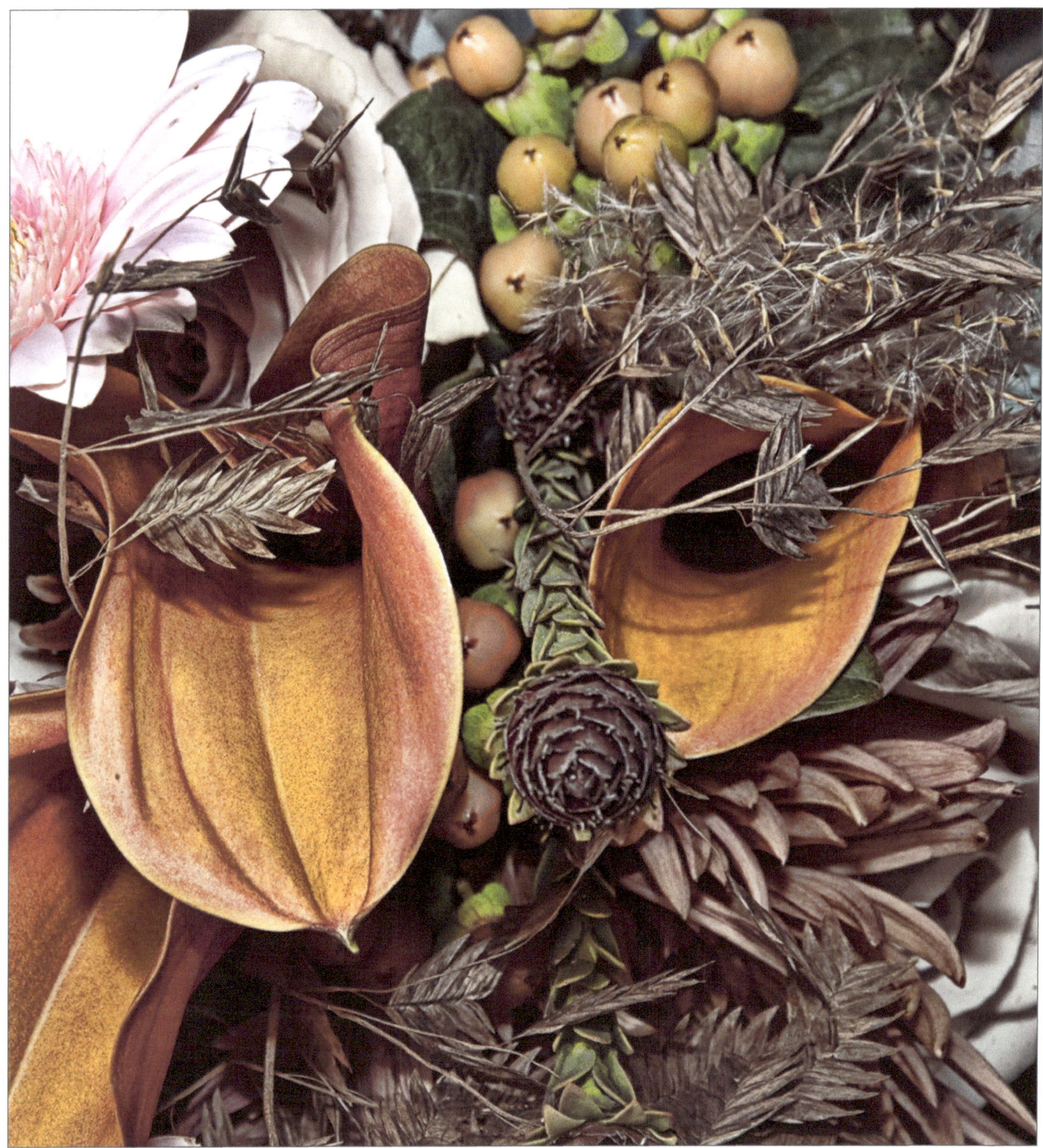

Natural. Cala lillies, color, natural elements from your garden and forest hikes—berries, leaves, moss, pinecones. You can bring your own special color and texture creativity to your wedding floral designs.

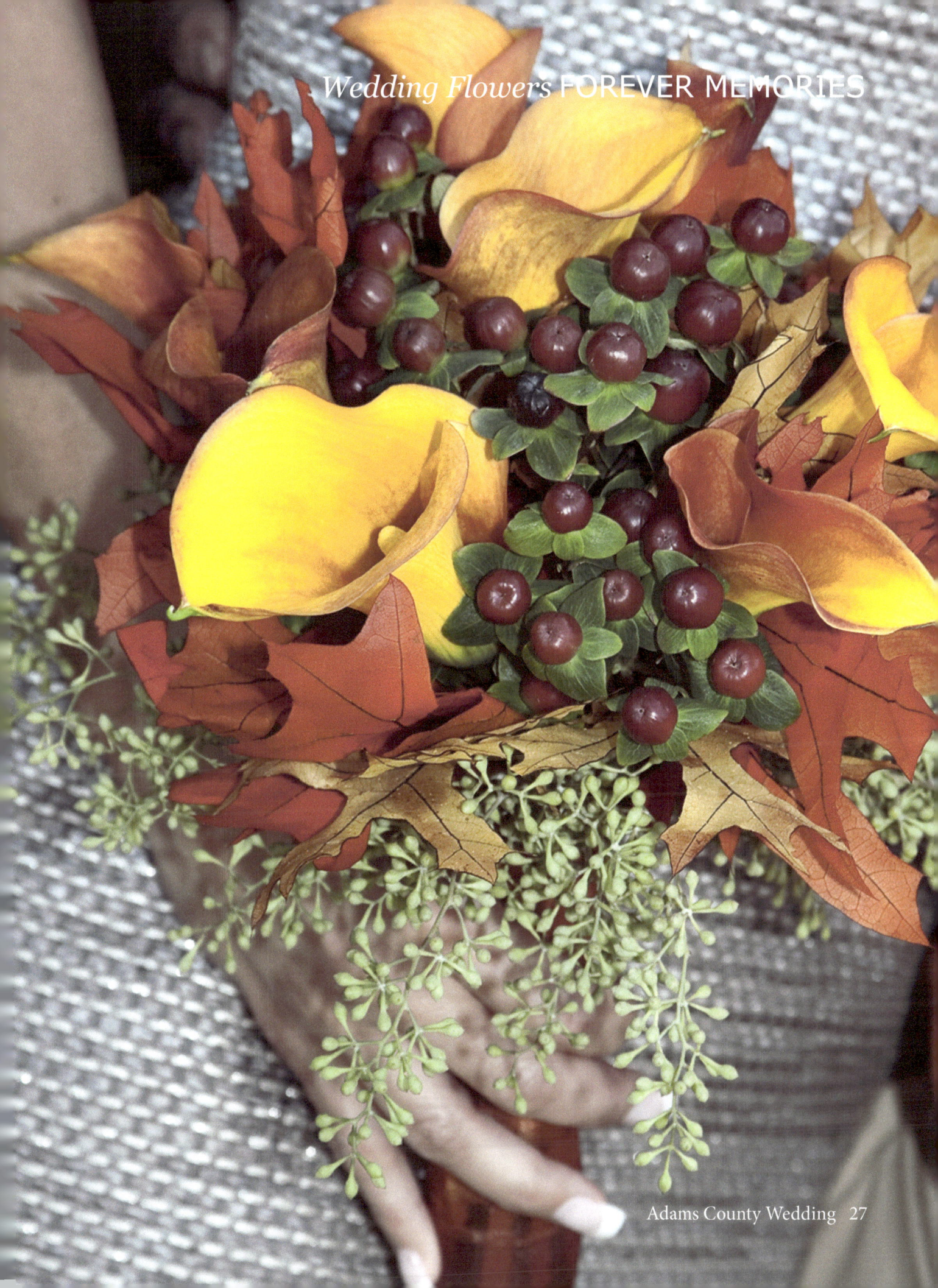

Wedding Design Theme PINK & BLING

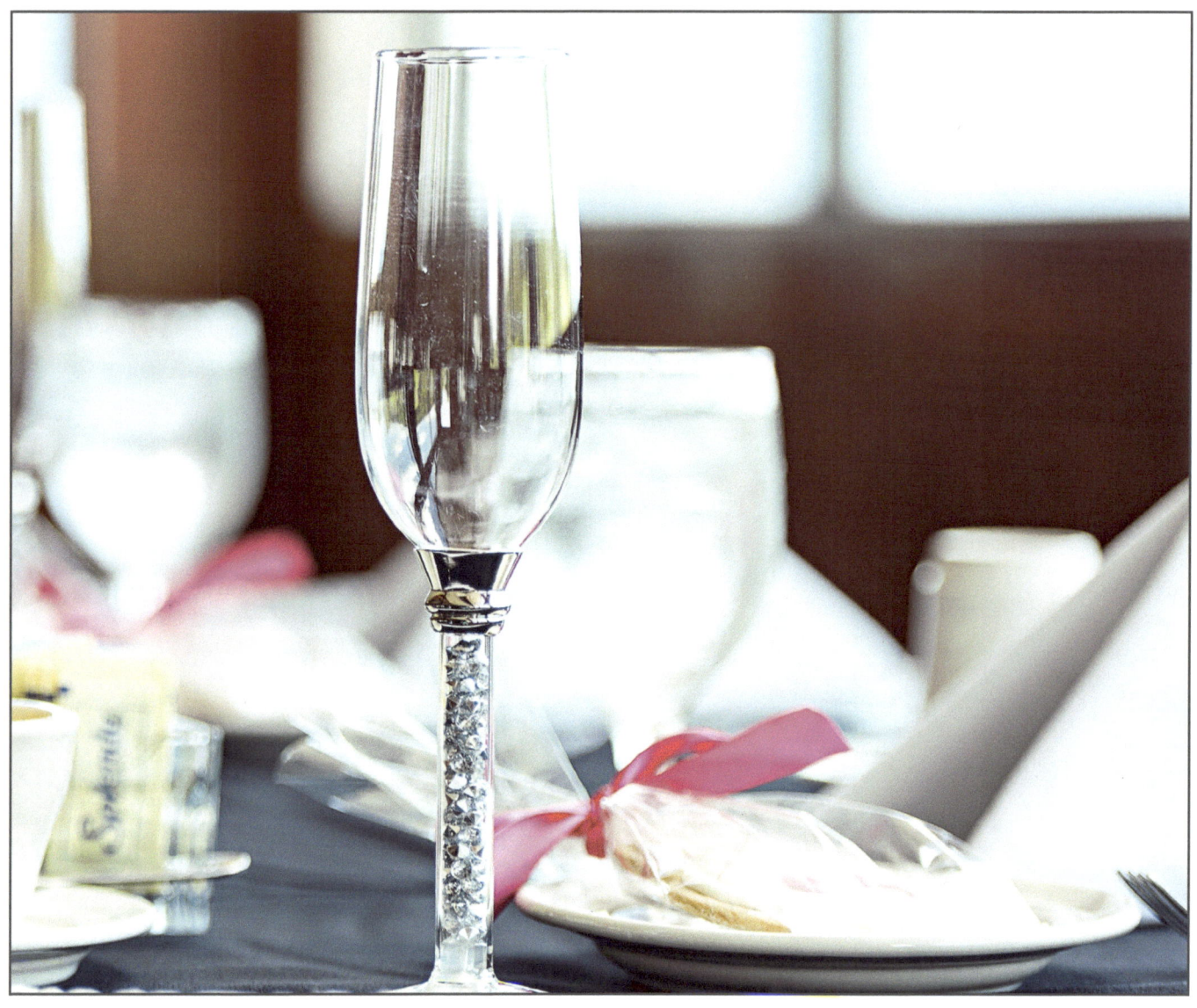

Photographed by Engin Caliskan

Adrian and Troy popped their formal black and white wedding theme with hot pink and crystal bling. They chose lush Gerbera daisies for the bouquets, in vases, on the cake—throughout the wedding and reception. The groomsmen wore hot pink neckties. Deep pink rose petals were used as an accent strewn on the tables and around the wedding cake. The table favors were tied with pink satin ribbon. "It's my favorite color so of course it had to be the color of my shoes!" Adrian told us. She found the rhinestones idea on Pinterest.

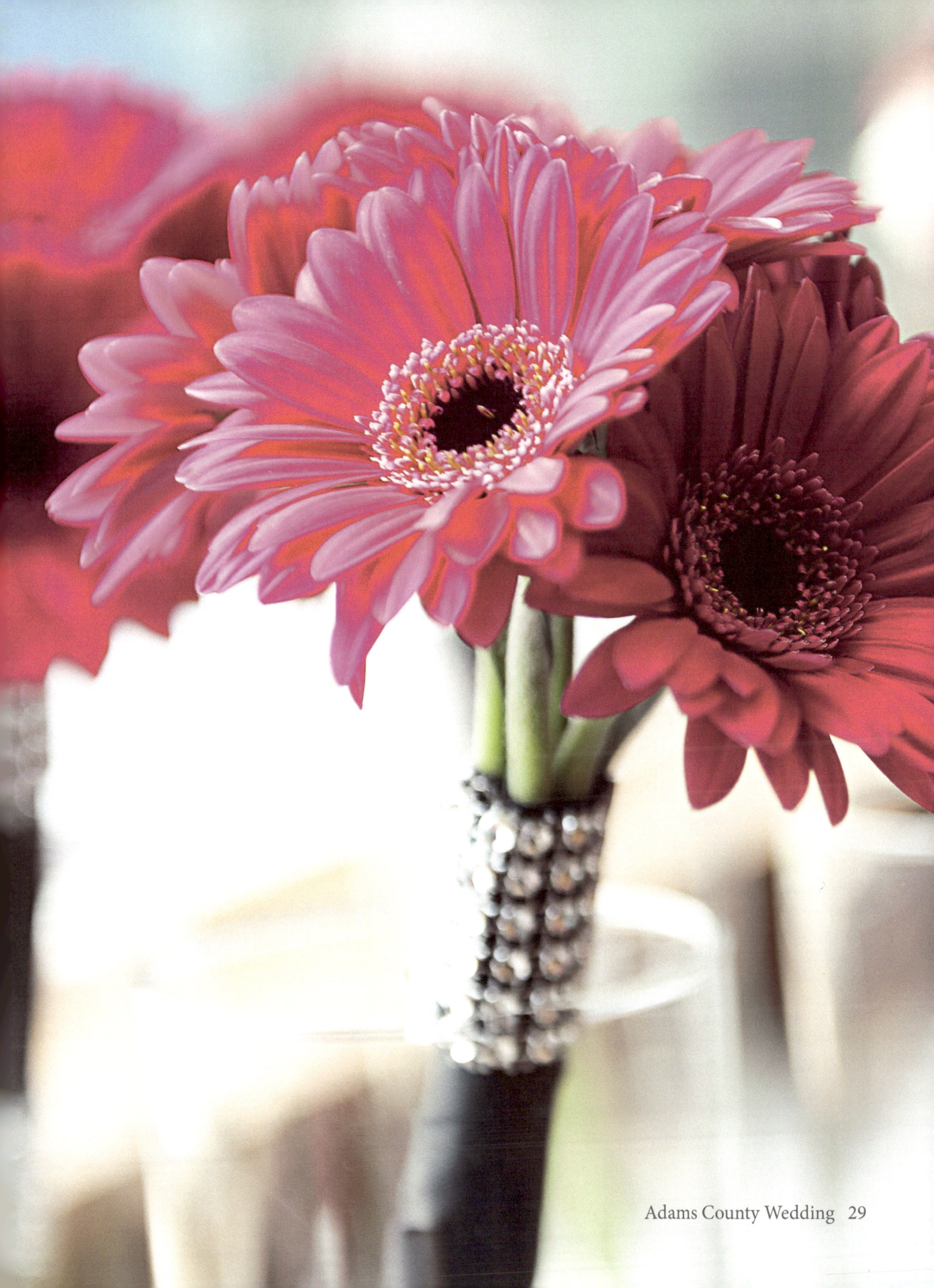

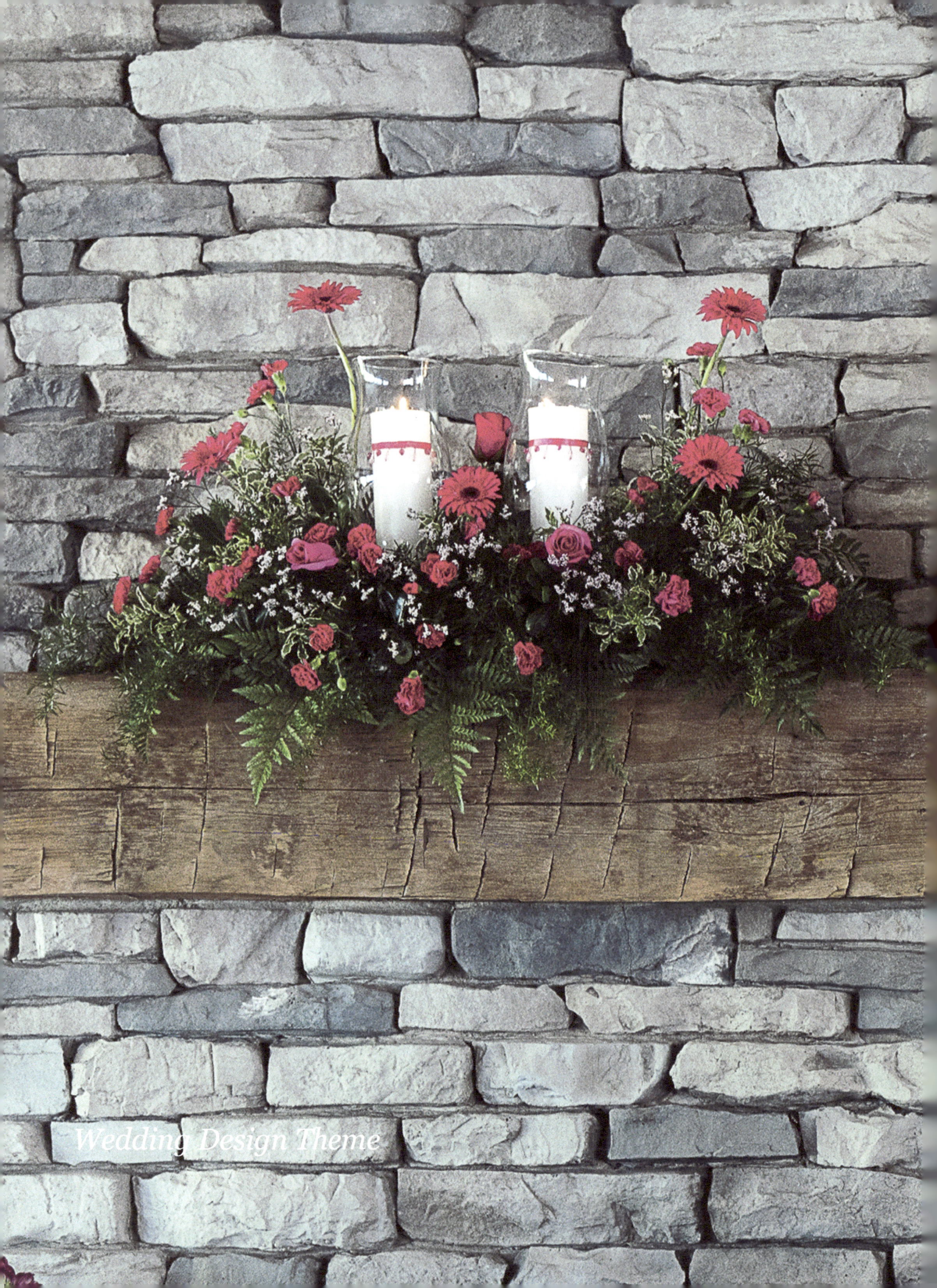

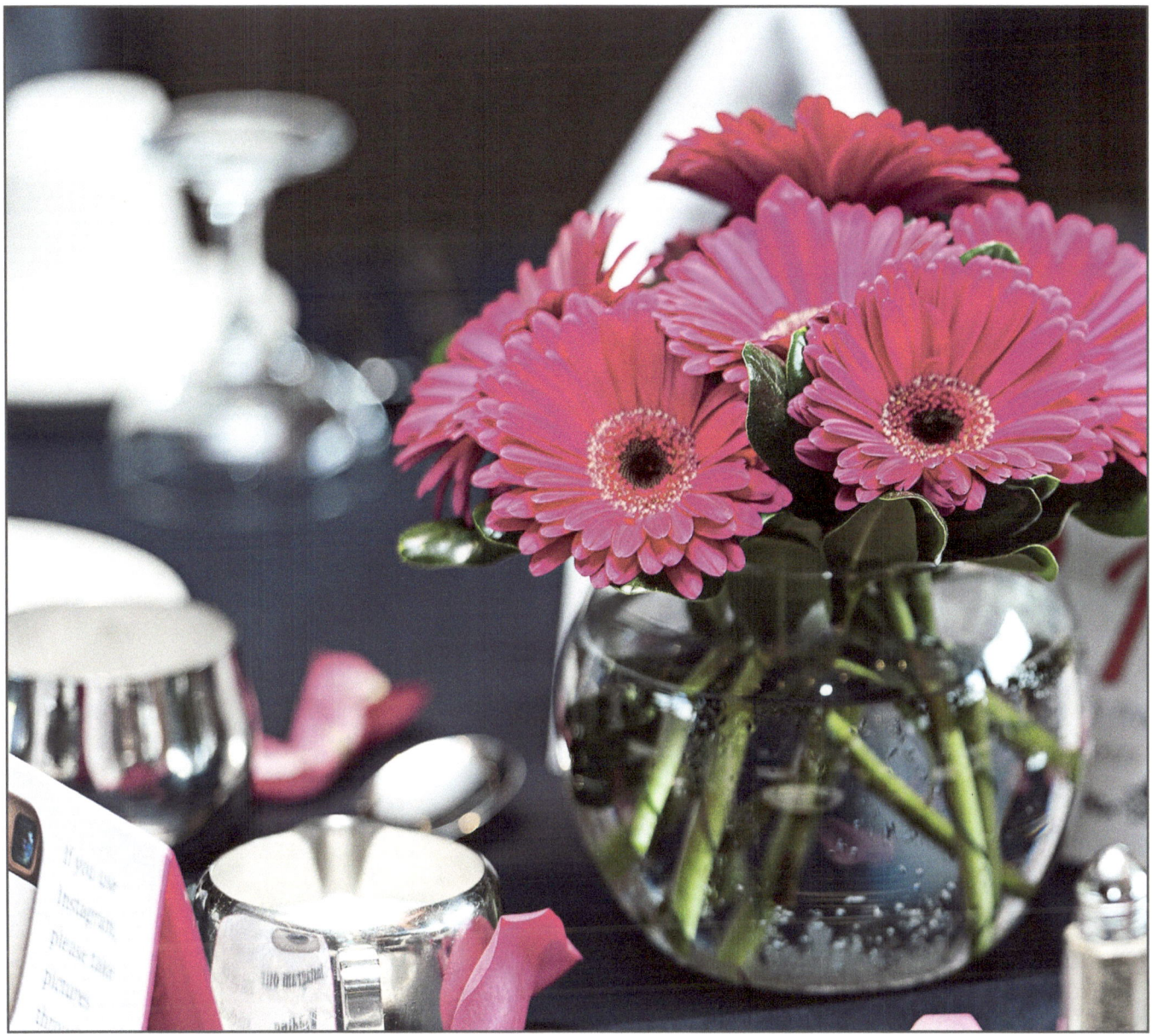

The reception location was the Liberty Mountain Resort and Conference Center, a great cavern of rough hewn beams with beautiful sky and mountain views. Coming from Maryland, Adrian had fond memories of winter ski trips here with her family. "It was also a huge bonus that they had a hotel for our traveling guests," she explained. The Flower Boutique placed crystal vases of fuscia daisies on the tables and arrangements around the room with candles and photos of the couple in ornate silver frames. Adrian called her design idea for their wedding "Formal and Fun." "We wanted to create a fun and inviting atmosphere and to enjoy the company of all of our guests."

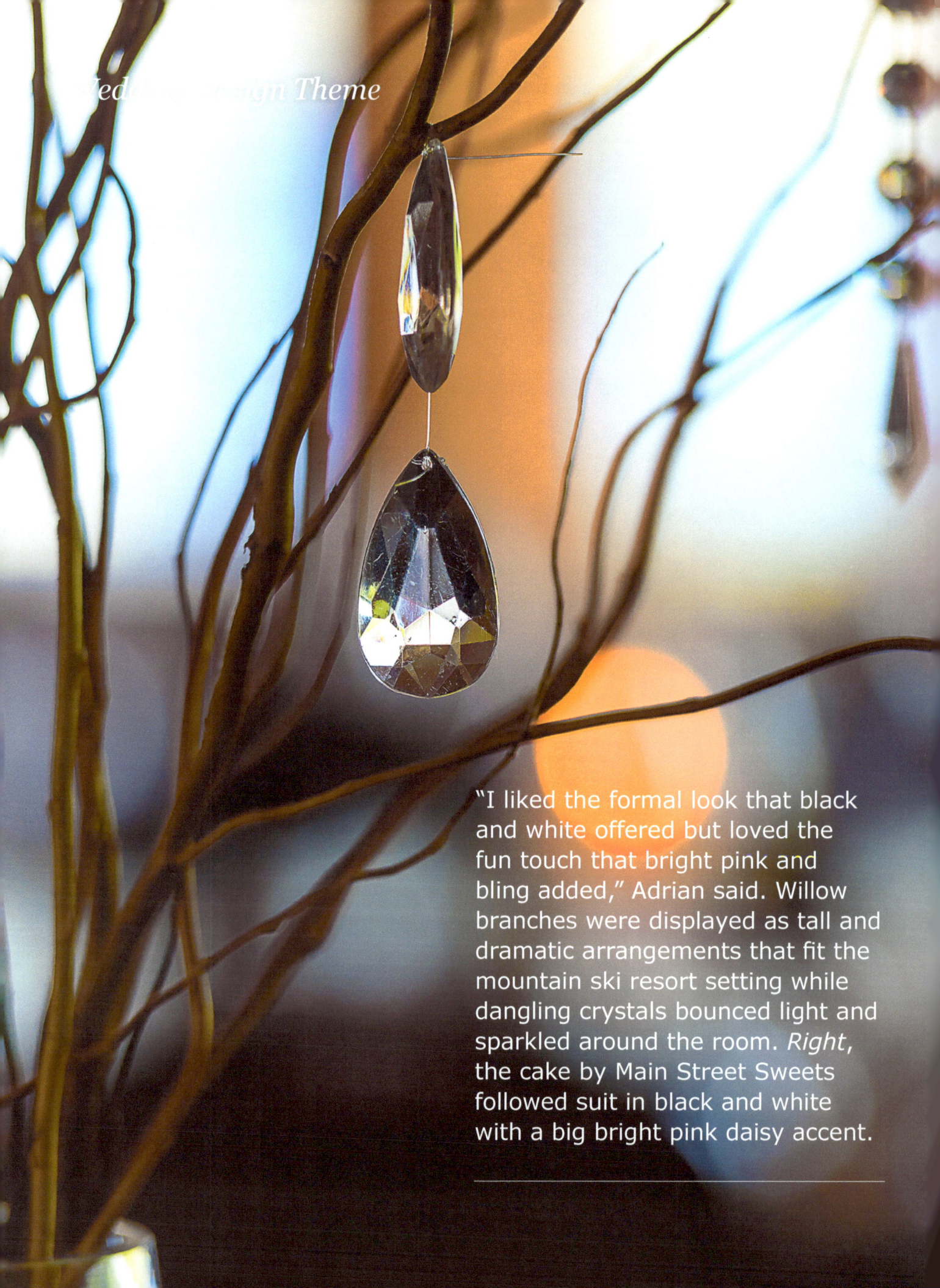

"I liked the formal look that black and white offered but loved the fun touch that bright pink and bling added," Adrian said. Willow branches were displayed as tall and dramatic arrangements that fit the mountain ski resort setting while dangling crystals bounced light and sparkled around the room. *Right*, the cake by Main Street Sweets followed suit in black and white with a big bright pink daisy accent.

"I loved being able to see the reception room all set up and decorated before anyone else was allowed to. It was such a nice moment with my Mom to be able to see everything come together. It was so beautiful!"

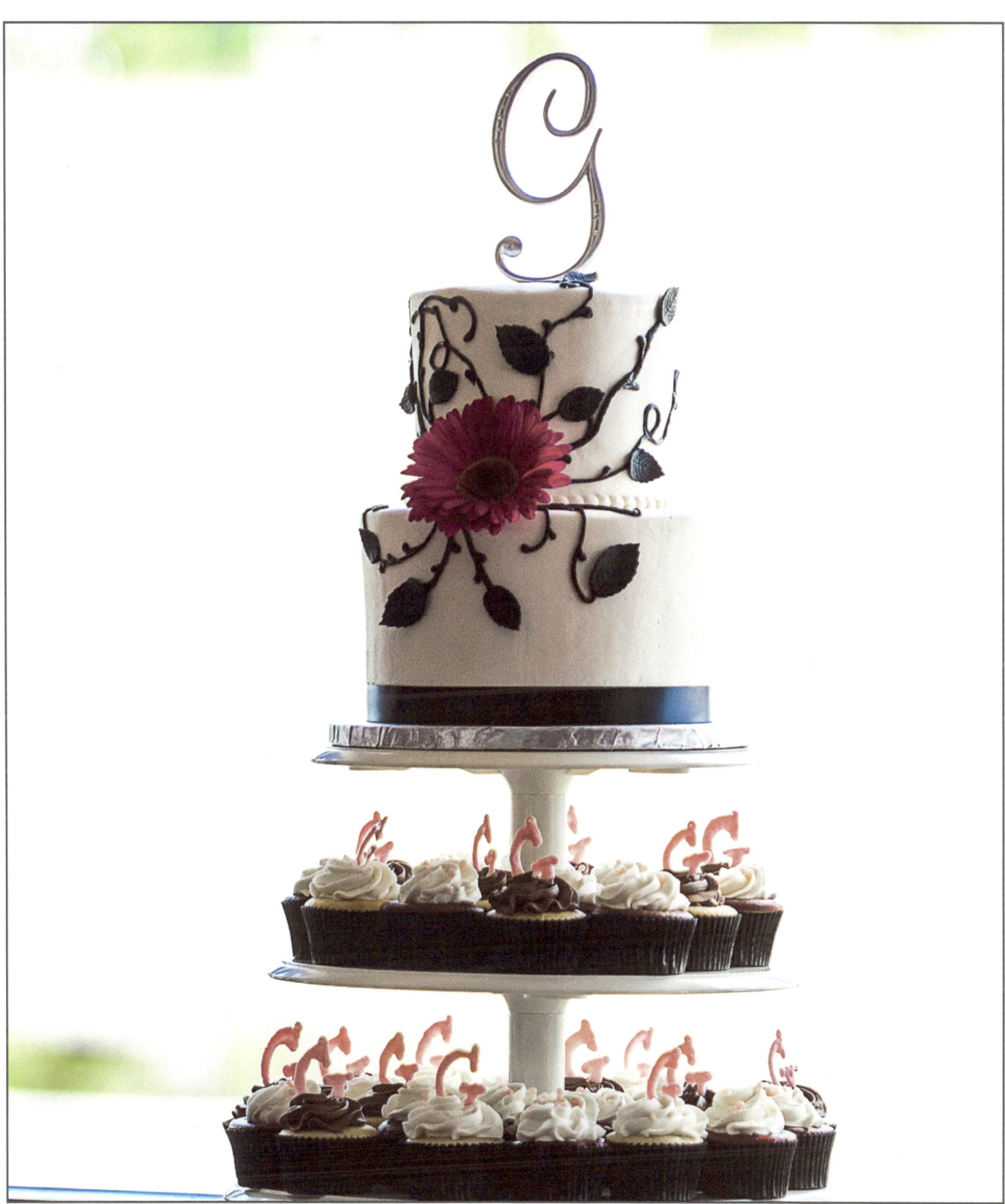

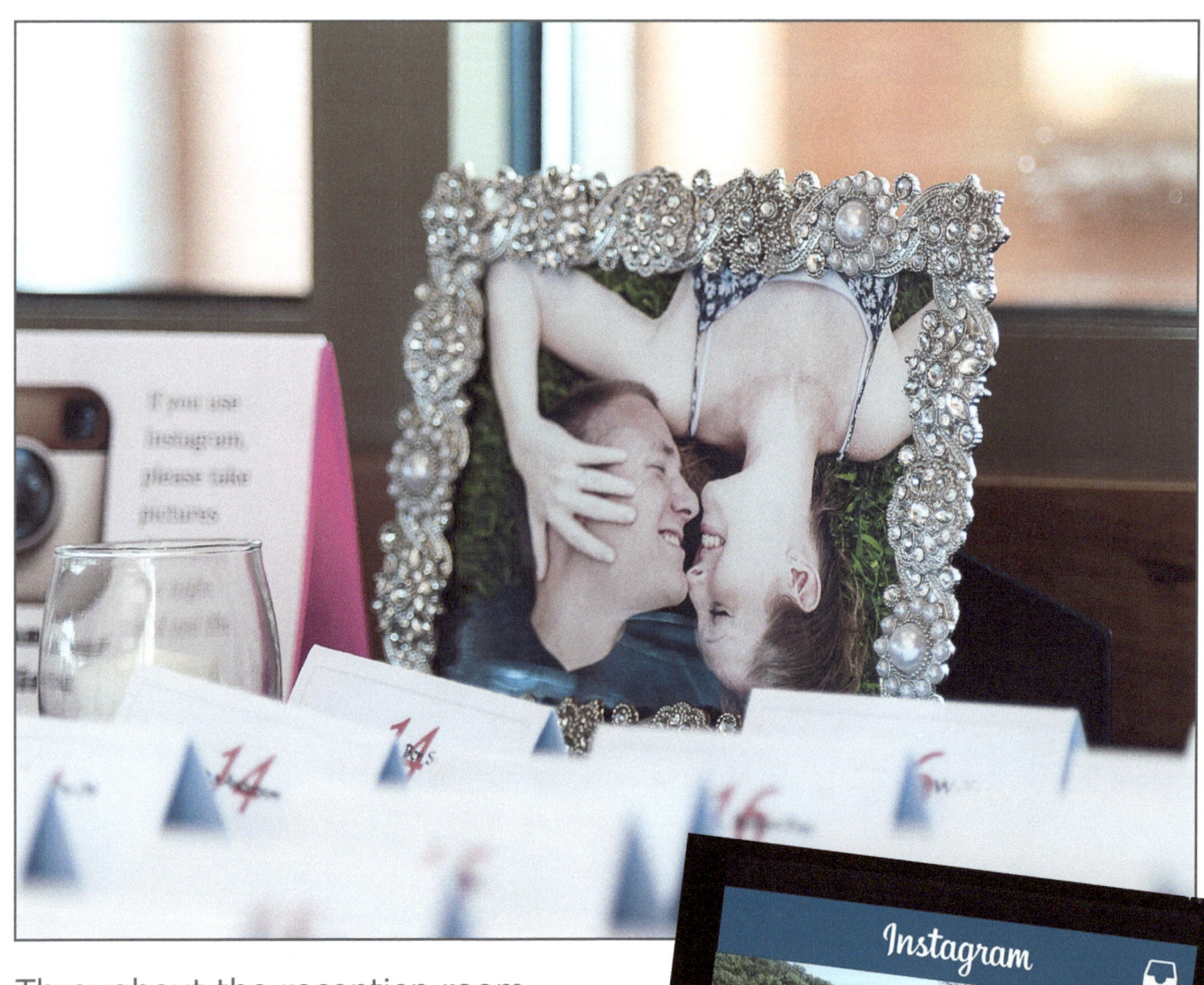

Throughout the reception room, photos of the couple were placed in sparkly frames along with signs encouraging guests to post their own wedding photos using a special hashtag. "Crowd sourcing some of our photos allowed us the opportunity to see the wedding from our guests' perspective! It was a nice addition to our photographer's pictures," Adrian said. We found them on Instagram and Facebook. Very smart.

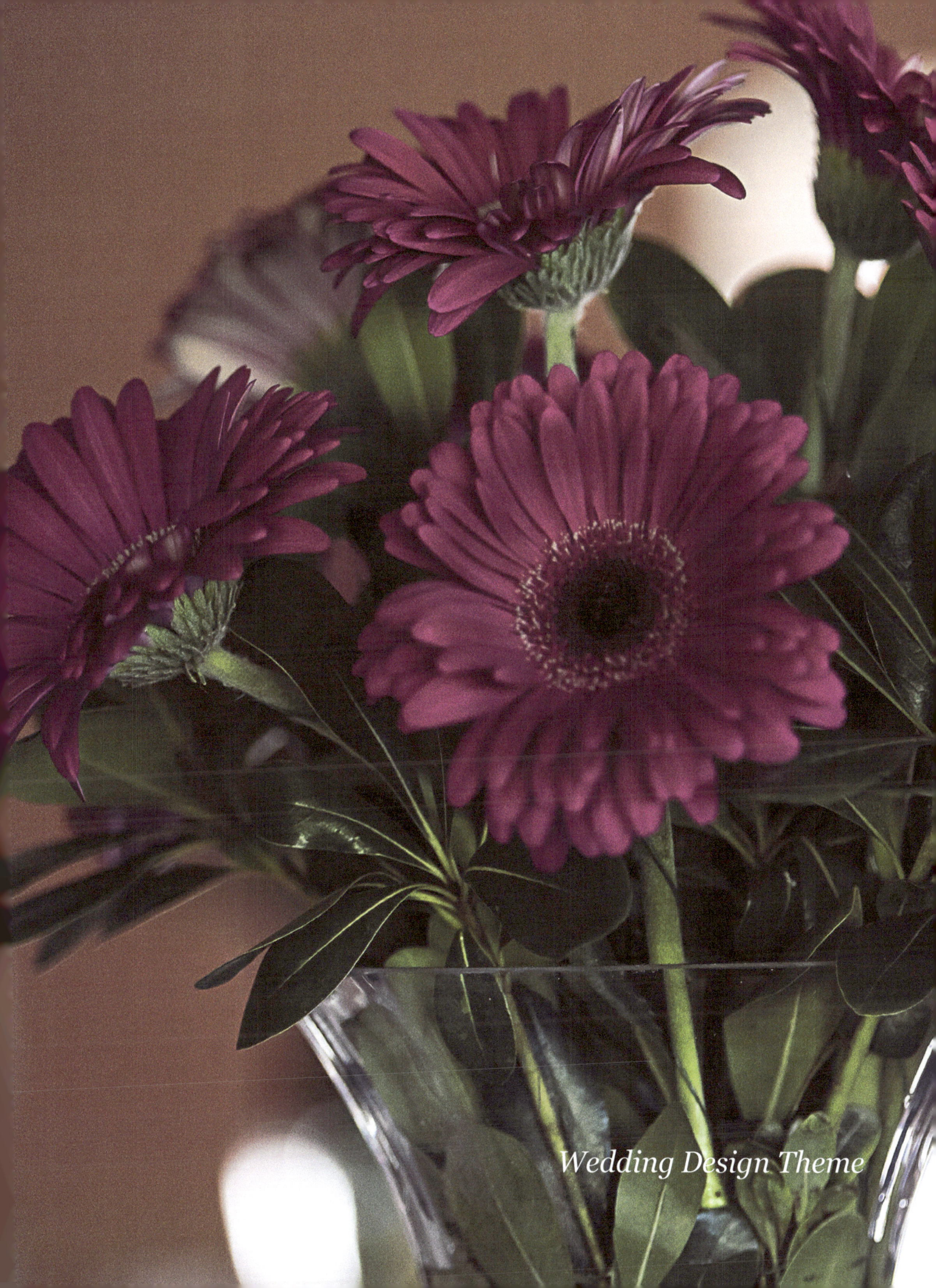

Wedding Design Theme

Reception A CLASSICALLY ELEGANT PARTY

Images were captured by Nina Ball and Krista Darrah-Spillman

Megan and Chris had a lovely traditional church wedding followed by a contemporary reception at Sidney Willoughby Run. The couple, both from Adams County, put a lot of thought into their choice. Megan explained, "The location and size, beautiful scenery, and reputation of the chef helped to make our decision." And they wanted it to be easy for their guests to travel from the church to the reception.

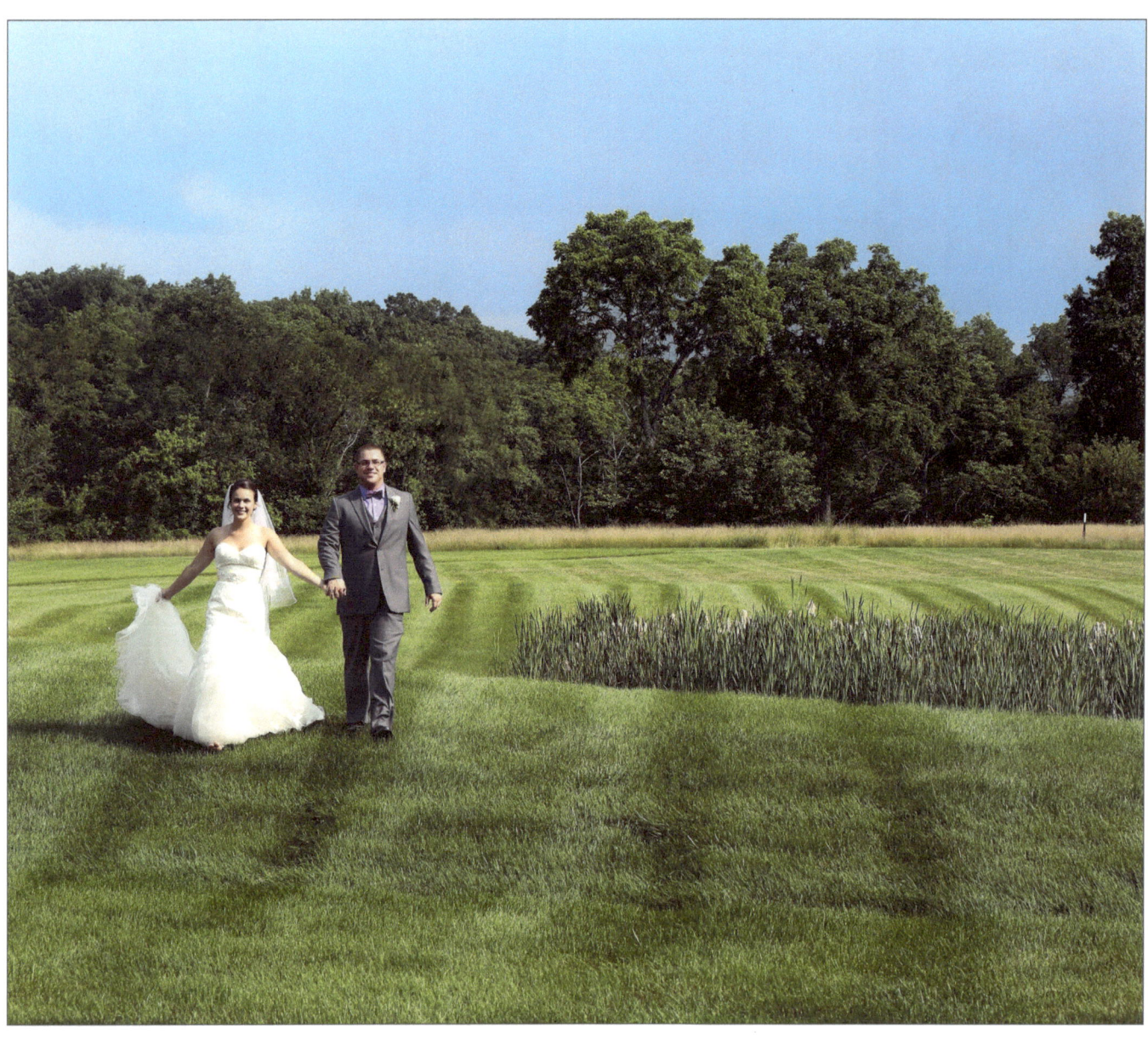

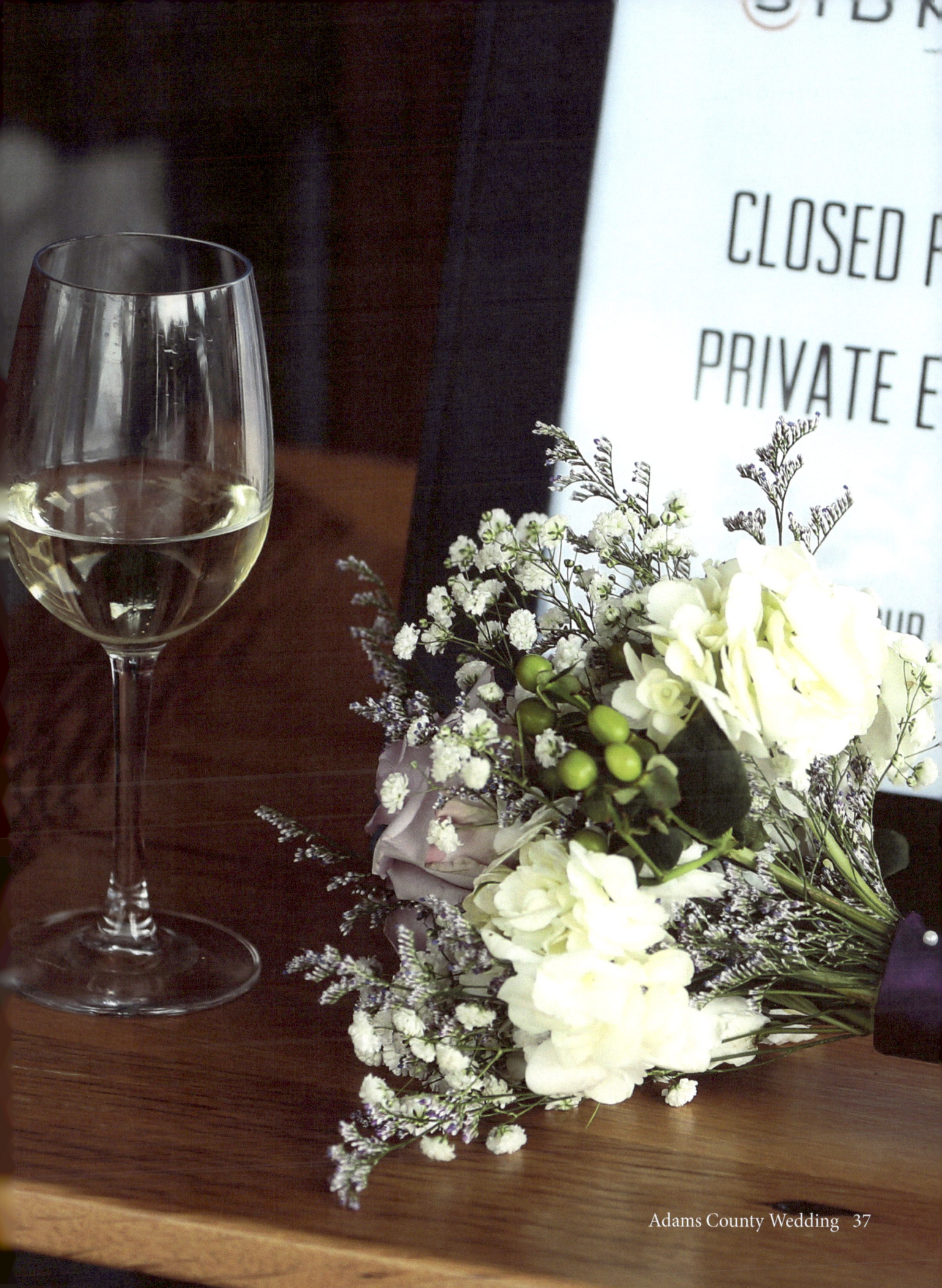

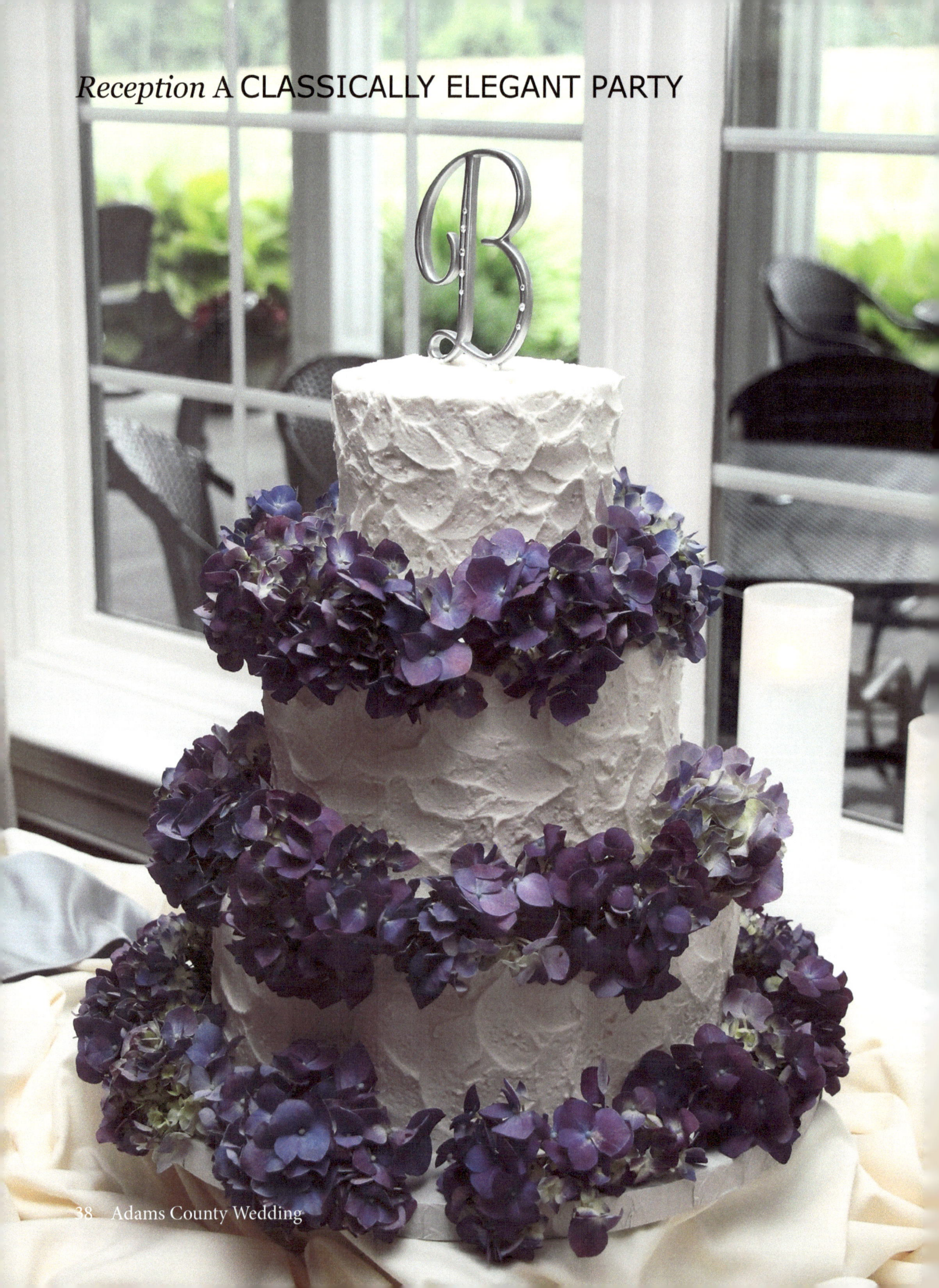

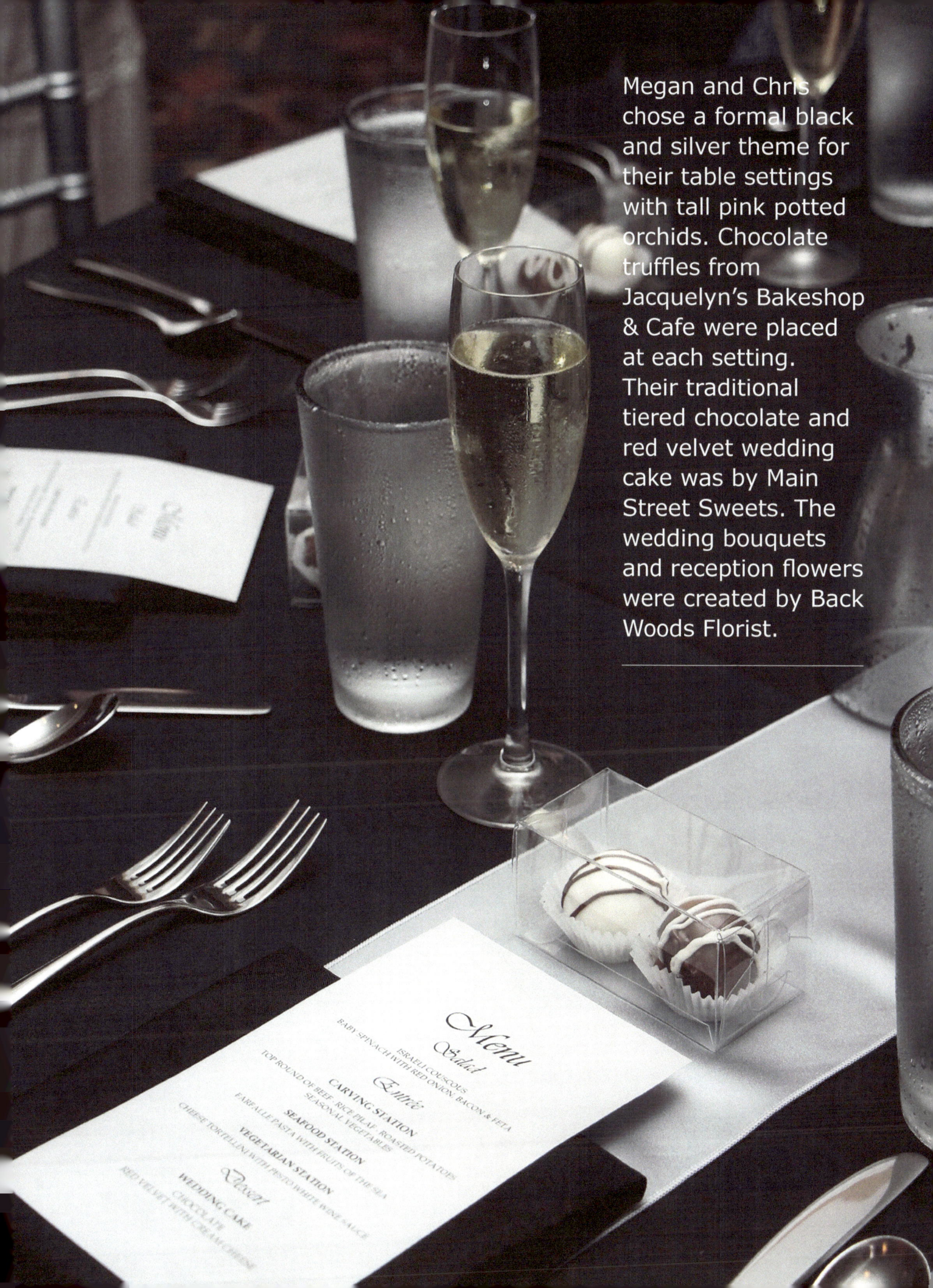

Megan and Chris chose a formal black and silver theme for their table settings with tall pink potted orchids. Chocolate truffles from Jacquelyn's Bakeshop & Cafe were placed at each setting. Their traditional tiered chocolate and red velvet wedding cake was by Main Street Sweets. The wedding bouquets and reception flowers were created by Back Woods Florist.

Menu

Salad
ISRAELI COUSCOUS
BABY SPINACH WITH RED ONION, BACON & FETA

Entrée

CARVING STATION
TOP ROUND OF BEEF · RICE PILAF · ROASTED POTATOES
SEASONAL VEGETABLES

SEAFOOD STATION
FARFALLE PASTA WITH FRUITS OF THE SEA

VEGETARIAN STATION
CHEESE TORTELLINI WITH PESTO WHITE WINE SAUCE

Dessert
WEDDING CAKE
CHOCOLATE
RED VELVET WITH CREAM CHEESE

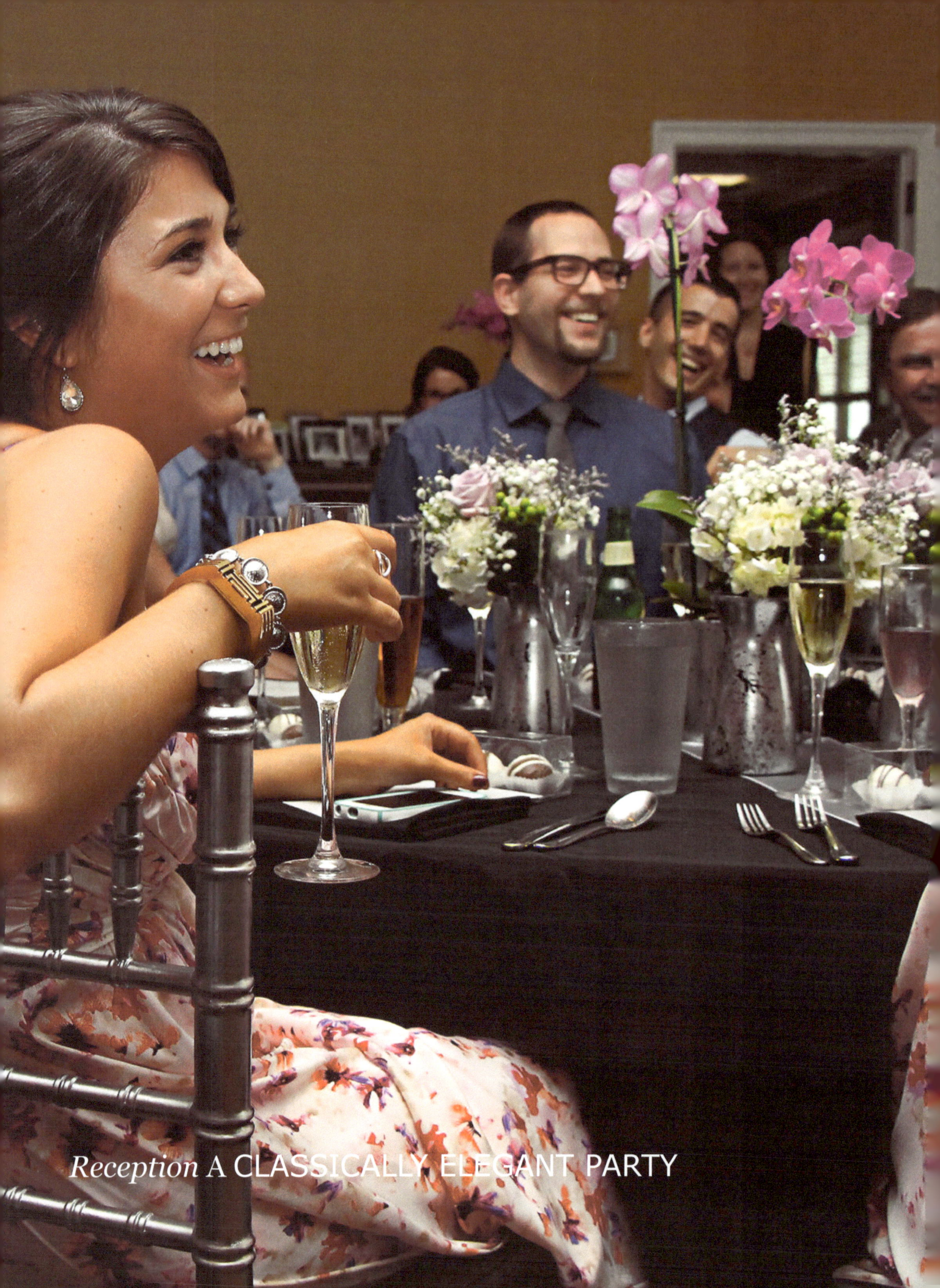

Reception A CLASSICALLY ELEGANT PARTY

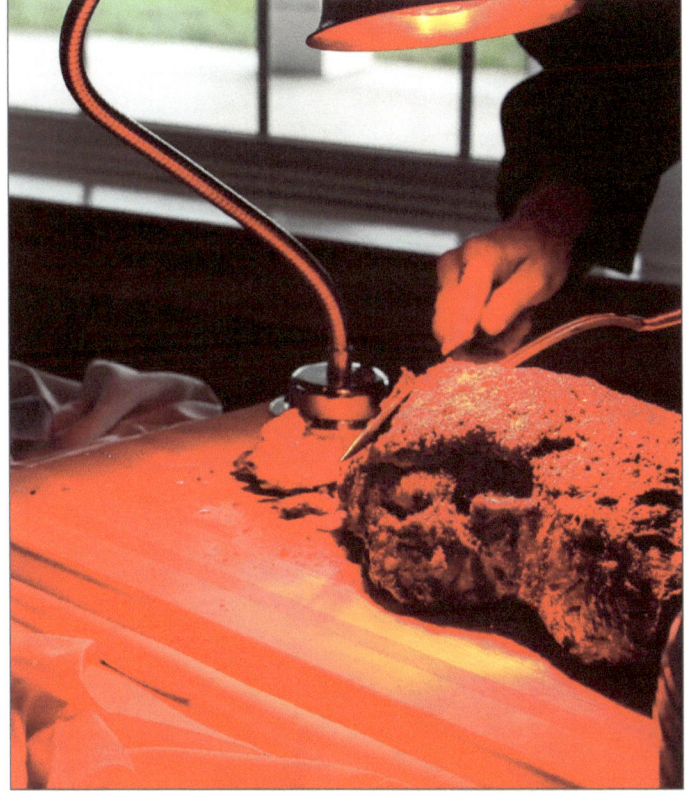

"Our guests were our number one priority. We wanted to be sure that they were going to enjoy themselves and feel the love between the two of us and the love and gratefulness that we felt towards all of them for celebrating our big day with us," Megan told us. For their wedding meal, Megan and Chris chose to have a variety of stations around the ballroom with hors d'oevres, salad, pasta, and carving table. The florist provided faux mercury glass vases on the tables for the bridesmaids to preserve their bouquets. An especially touching idea was the memory table, where photos of family members who could not be there were honored. Megan said, "To remind us that they were there—watching from heaven."

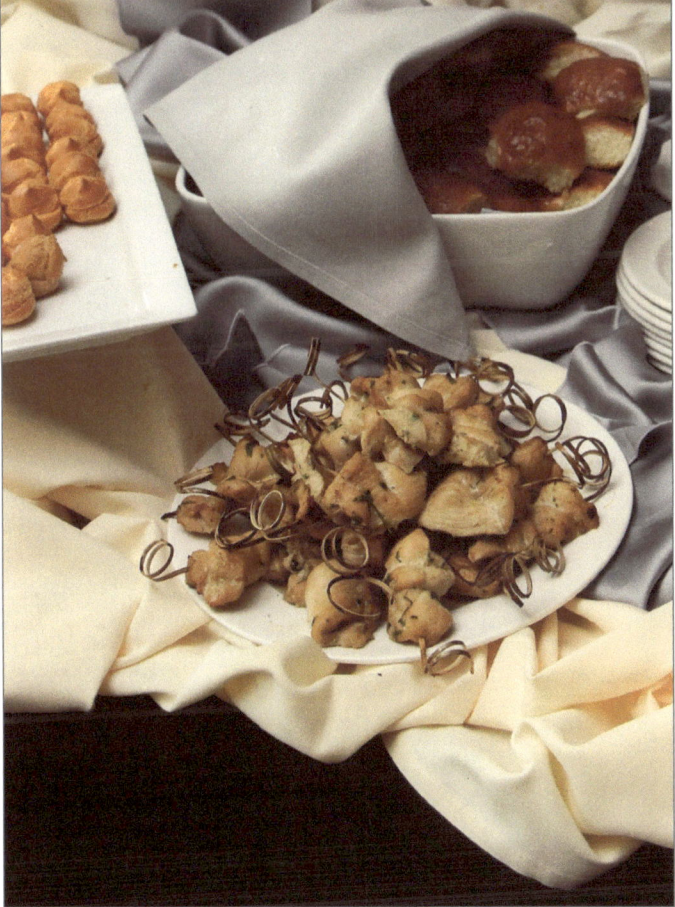

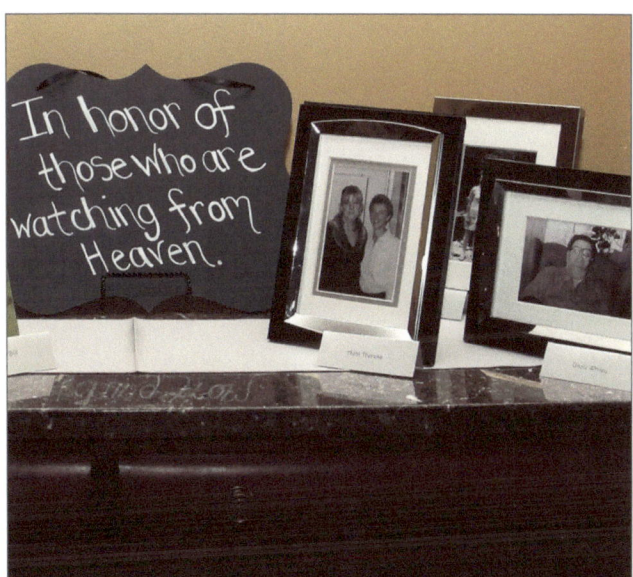

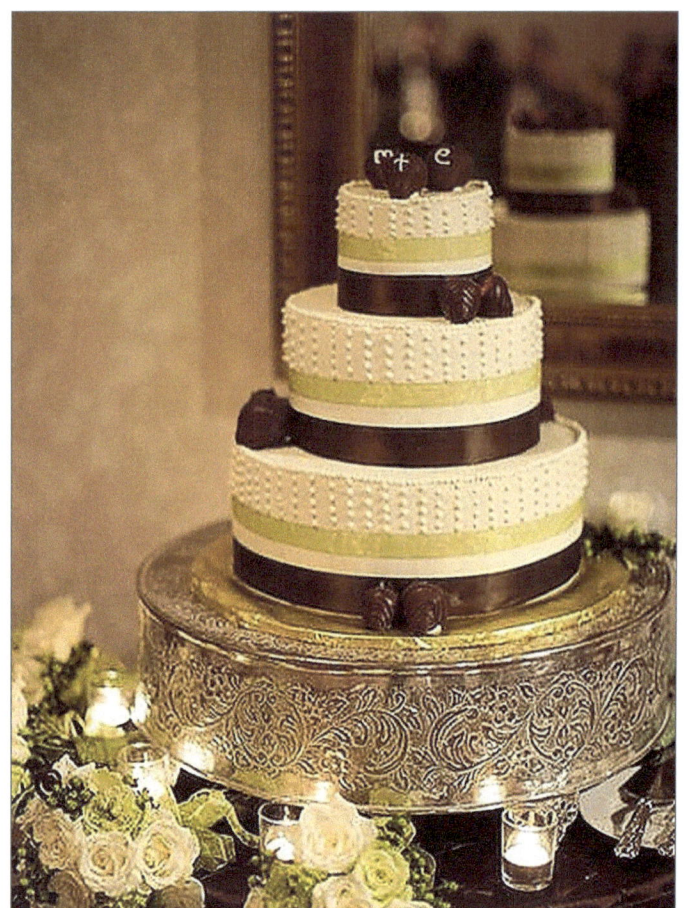

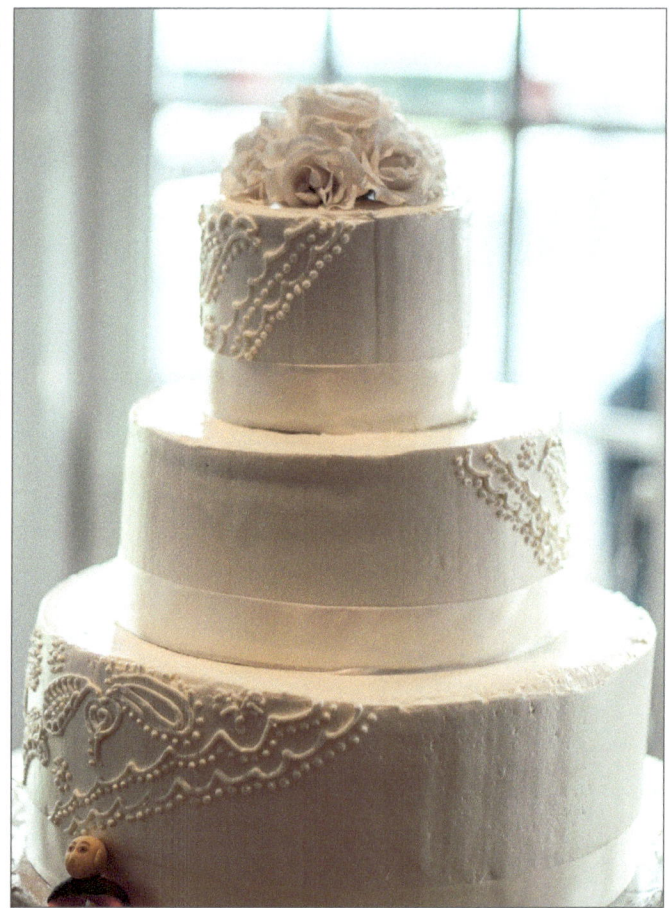

Classic.

There are no "rules" when it comes to choosing your wedding cake design but there are some classic styles. A tiered cake banded with satin, embelllished with swirls of sweet buttery icing and real (or sugar) flowers, for instance. The icing designs can reflect the lace of the gown or the paisley of the groom's attire. The top layer is traditionally whisked away to save for sharing on the first anniversary.

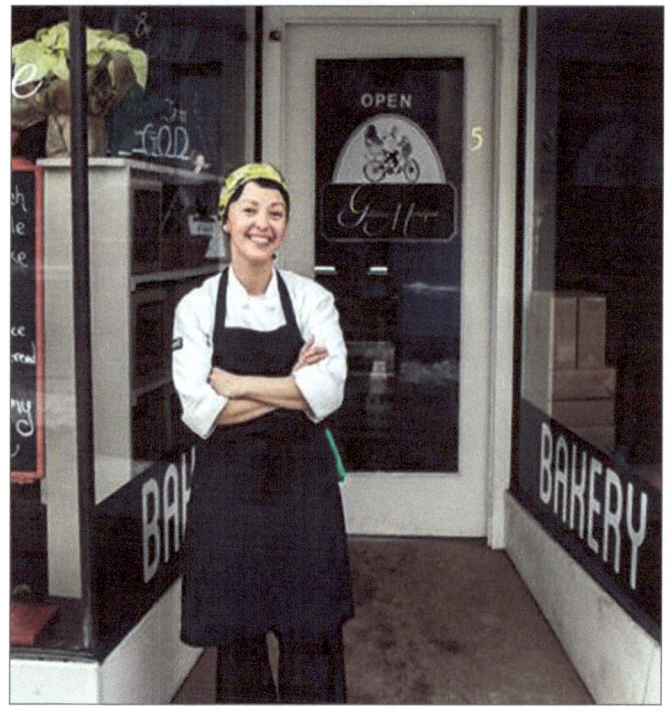

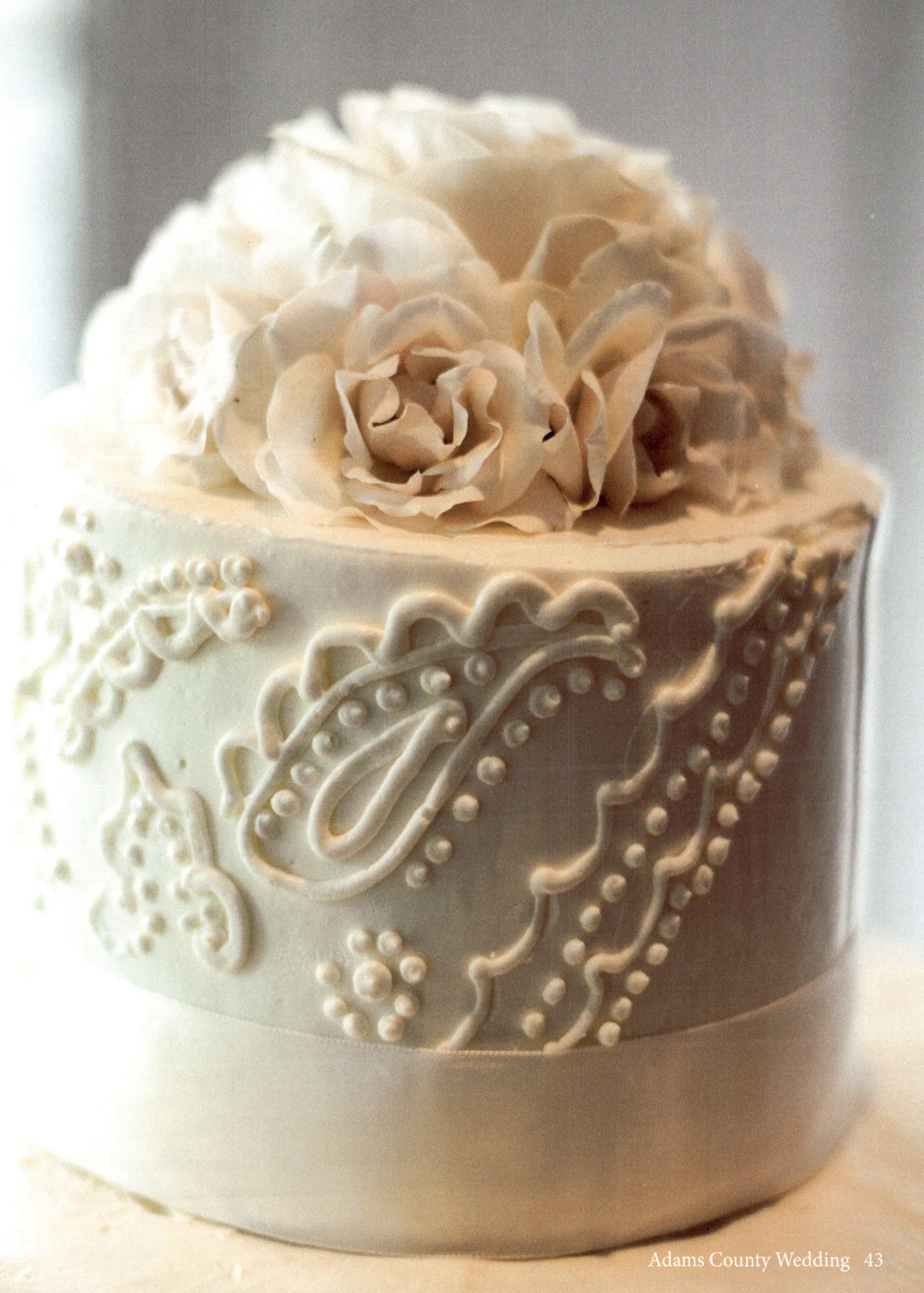

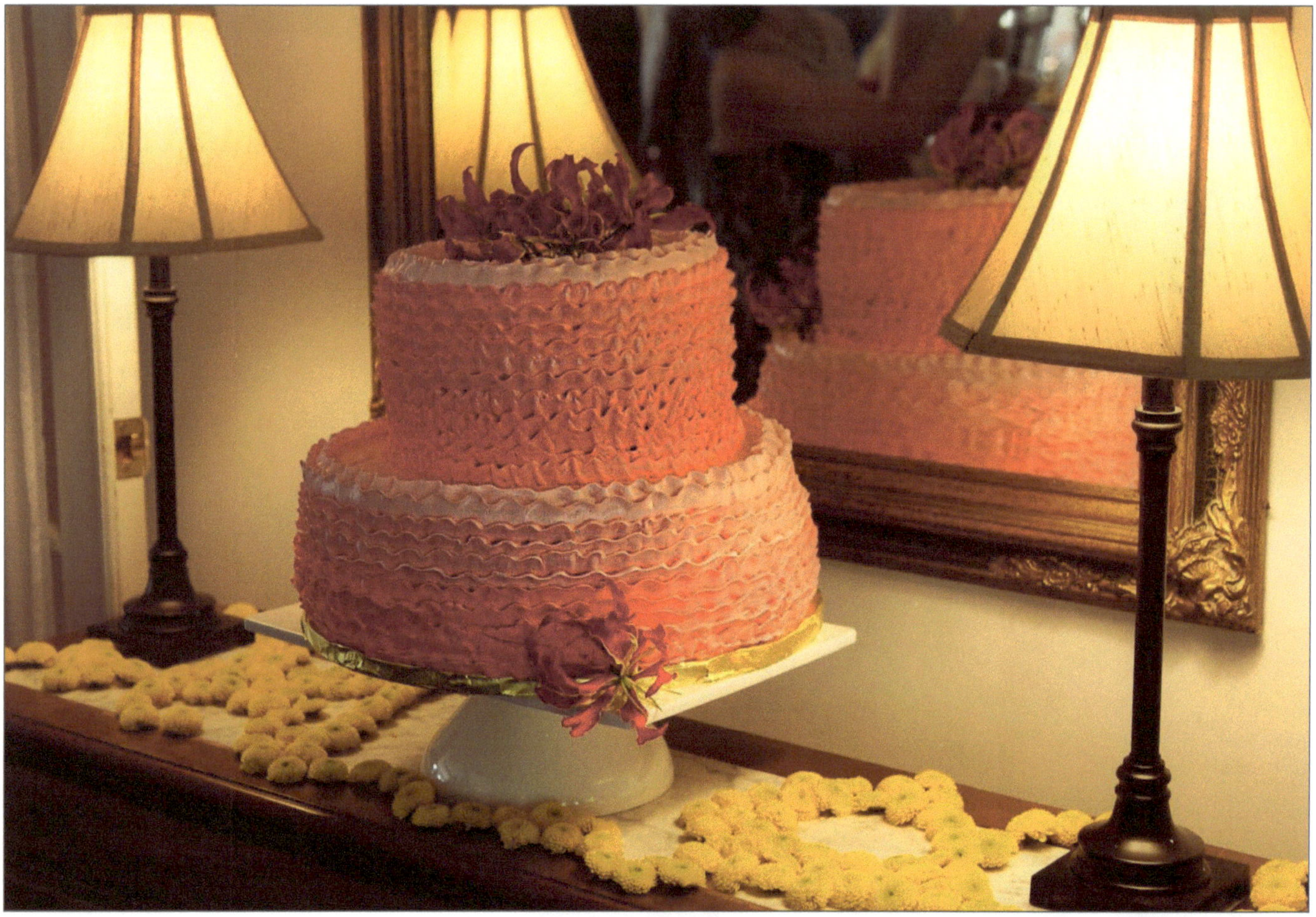

Color. Monique says, "Colorful cakes are fun, make a statement, and reflect the personality of a bride and groom." Icing can be smooth or luxuriously ruffled. And more couples are choosing to share wedding cupcakes instead of a tiered cake, with a small cake for the cutting ceremony. A duplicate small cake is often made and saved for their anniversary.

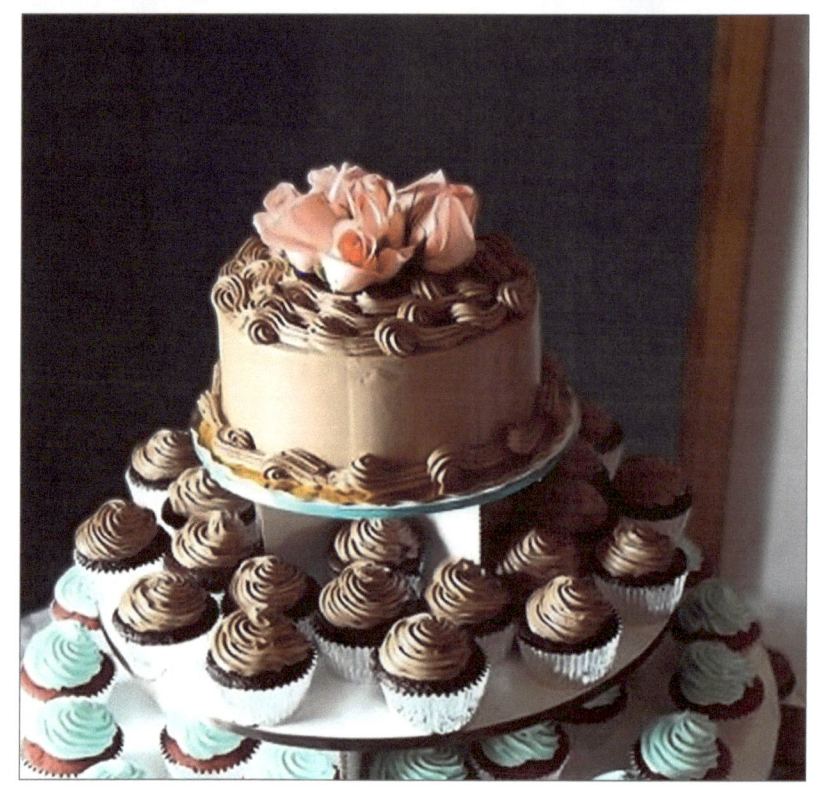

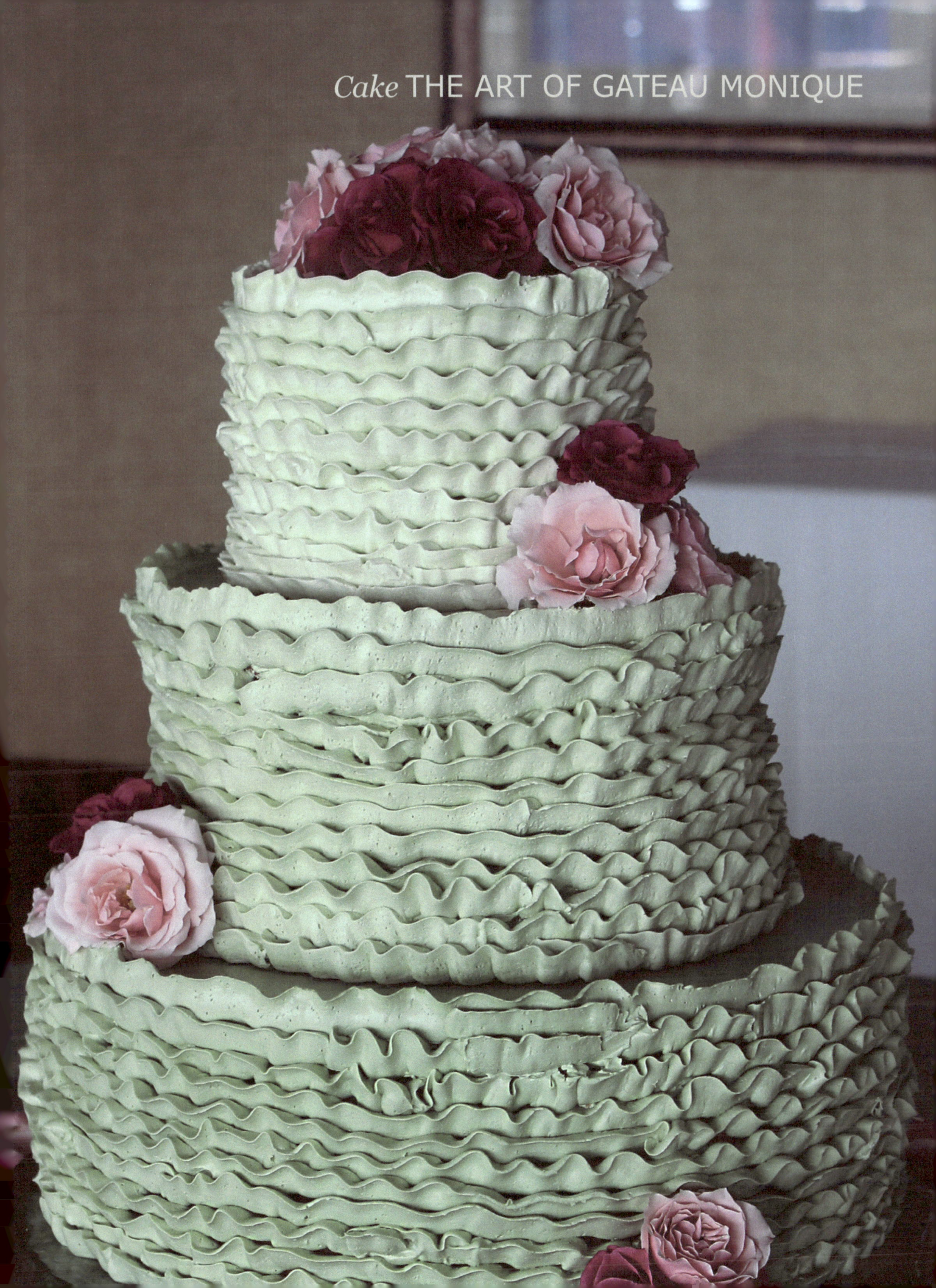

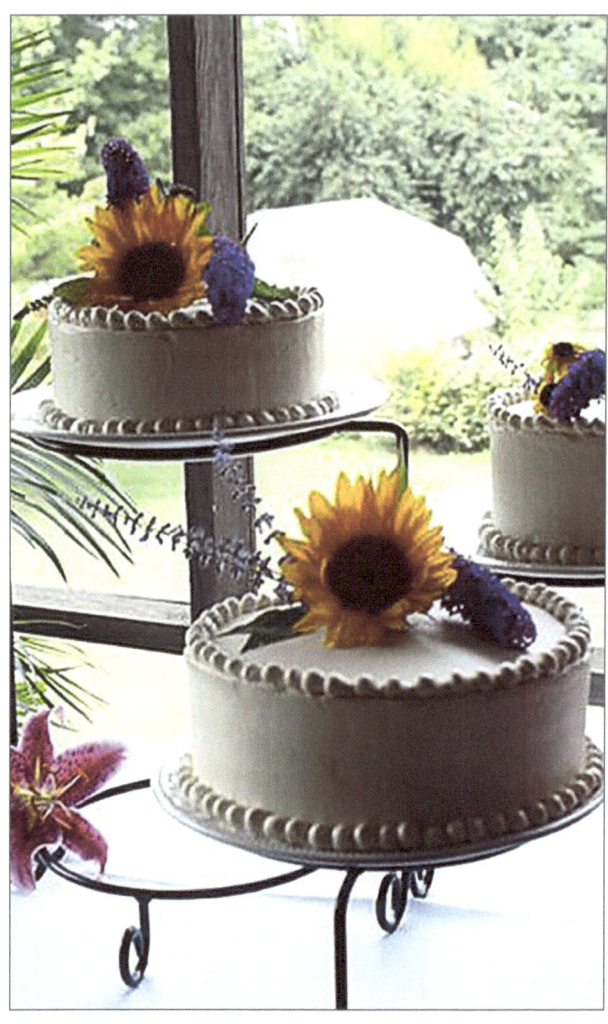

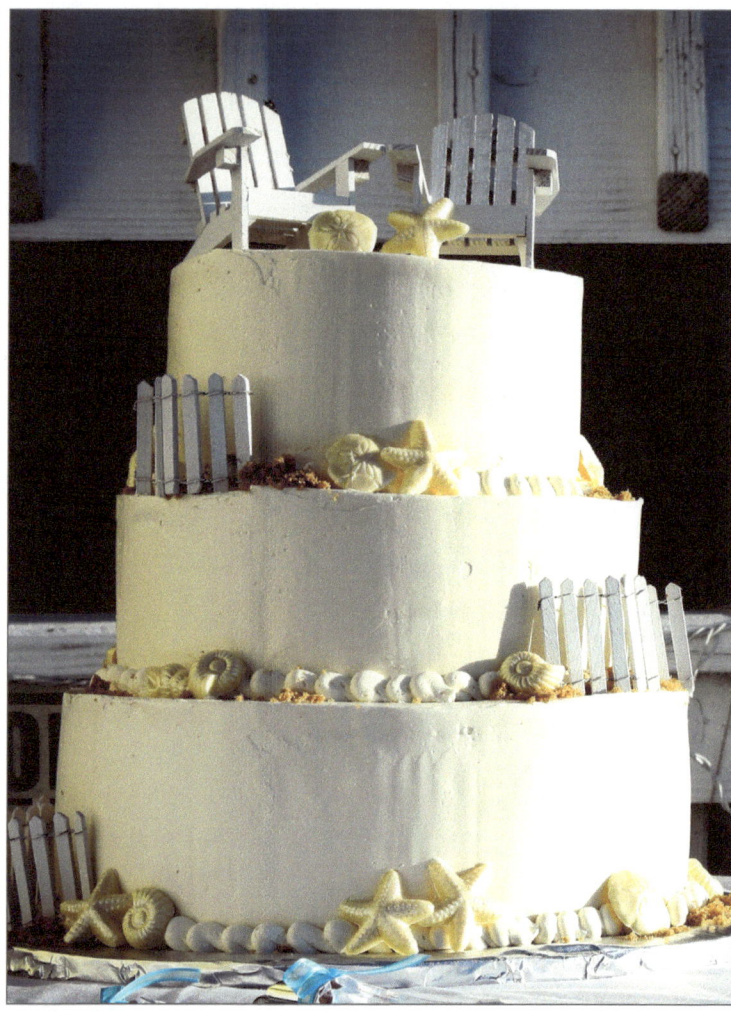

Afton Huntley Photography

White. Who says a white wedding cake can't be fun. Monique made a modern and creative cake with sea shells, dune fences and Adirondack chairs for a special beach wedding. Or decorate your cake with big, bright flowers. Instead of a single tiered cake, present several smaller cakes, then surround your cake with a variety of dessert treats, chocolates, fruit, candies.

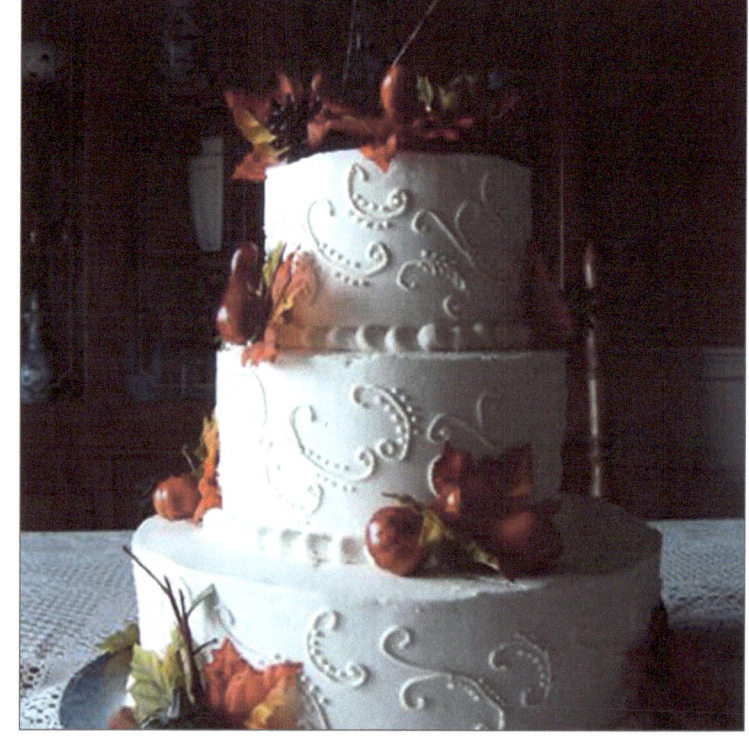

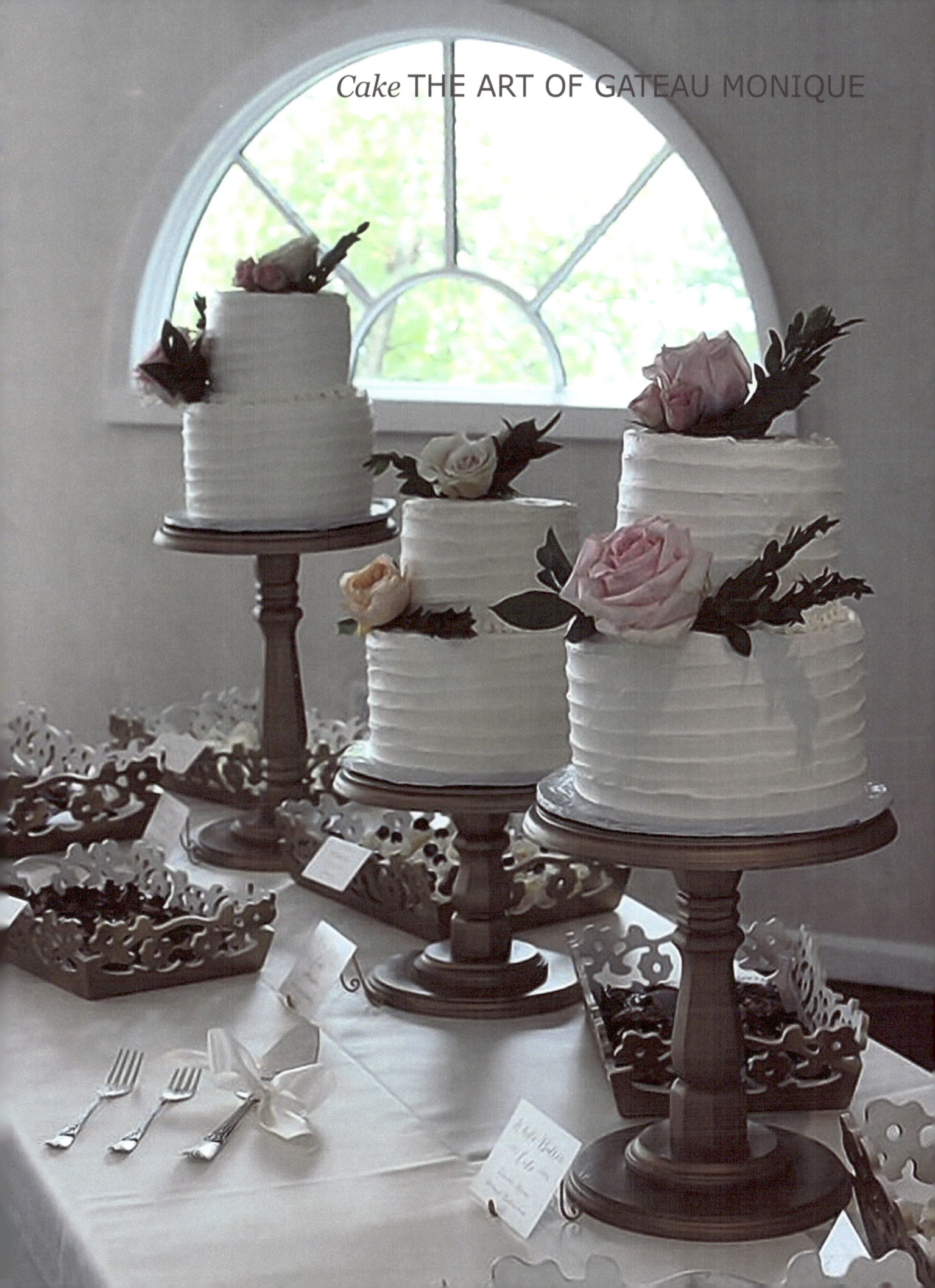

Favors & Gifts FROM THE HEART

When David and I were dating, I saved every rose he gave me and put them in a crock with spices to make a fragrant potpourri.

For our wedding reception, I made up pint Ball jars with a scoop of the sweet rose potpourri to share with our family and friends. Before the ceremony, I placed a jar at each table setting.

A ribbon and a note was tied to every jar with the story of the roses which ended with the words, "I hope these roses bring to you the happiness that they have brought to me."

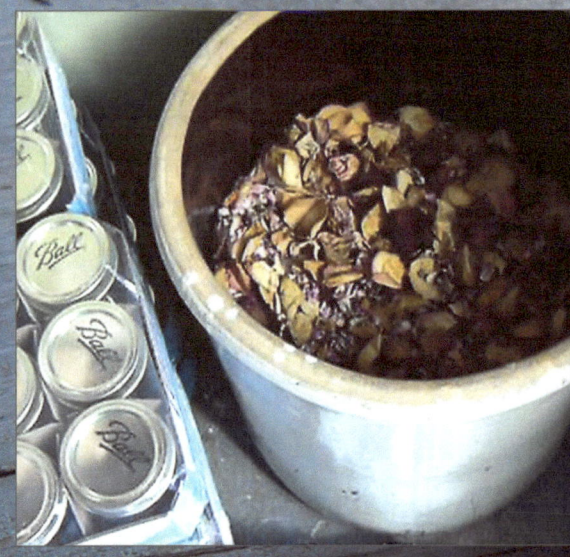

The Directory IN THIS ISSUE

Adams County Wedding

Volume 1, Number 1, Fall 2015

PUBLICATION INFORMATION

Digital Magazine
All current issues of the *Adams County Wedding* are available for FREE as a PDF download online at http://adamscountywedding.com

Printed Magazine
Free. If you are mentioned in an issue, we would be glad to send you a print magazine at no cost. Please email your name and mailing address with your request and issue date to susan@adamscw.com

Purchase single copies. Current or back print issues are available at Amazon.com. Just search "Adams County Wedding" or use the link at the end of each issue description on the magazine website http://adamscw.com. Individual print magazines are available for about $12.95 plus shipping. At times, Amazon offers promotional discounts, free shipping, and some issues, containing more pages, may be priced at a slightly higher cost.

Purchase wholesale. If you are a business, you can register with Amazon's CreateSpace and bulk purchase the *Adams County Wedding* print magazine at wholesale. You can then give away the magazine as a premium to your customers or resell them at your business, as you choose. Go to http://createspace.com and search for "reseller account" or use this link to go directly to the Amazon CreateSpace Reseller Application. https://goo.gl/djSyiV

Advertising in the *Adams County Wedding*
The founding concept of this magazine is to document Adams County life through stories and photography without the bias and clutter that may result from serving advertising. We do not accept advertising, in-kind trade of goods, free products nor free services in exchange for story coverage. Bridal couples agree to let us use their photographs, photographers and services let us show their work without charge. We seek great stories, creative and interesting ideas, and cover our experience in the magazine as our conscience dictates—without the influence of any kind of financial arrangements. *You won't find something in our magazine because someone paid for it to be there.*

Our mission is to document those simple things around us that we love, the special people we have come to know, the extraordinary places, activities, food, history, events and local traditions we discover living in Adams County, Pennsylvania. In fulfilling that mission, *Adams County Wedding* does highlight many local businesses and organizations, both in our magazine and online in our social media. In this Fall 2015 issue alone, we have credited 18 local businesses, venues or organizations. No guarantee, however, is implied or implicit for any of the businesses mentioned; we are simply reporting, sharing stories, ideas and resources. We hope you enjoy reading about these families and businesses and that by sharing their stories we are having a positive impact in our community.

We welcome your press releases and announcements to alert us to your news and upcoming events. We welcome your feedback and responses to our editorial content and policies. Please send them to susan@adamscw.com.

Submit Your Wonderful Wedding Stories Here!
If you would like to submit your *Adams County Wedding* ideas to us — engagement stories, flower designs, venues, wedding photos, honeymoon, anything related to celebrating your wedding, we would love to see them and might even contact you to publish your story! Email: susan@adamscw.com